Religious Change in America

SOCIAL
TRENDS
IN THE
UNITED
STATES

Editors
James A. Davis
John Modell

Committee on Social Indicators
Social Science Research Council

Religious Change in America

Andrew M. Greeley

Harvard University Press
Cambridge, Massachusetts
London, England
1989

Library of Congress Cataloging-in-Publication Data

Greeley, Andrew M., 1928–
   Religious change in America / Andrew M. Greeley.
     p. cm.—(Social trends in the United States)
   Bibliography: p.
   Includes index.
   ISBN 0–674–75840–4 (alk. paper)
   1. United States—Religion—1945–   I. Title. II. Series.
BL2525.G73   1989
306'.6'0973—dc19
                          88–29417
                             CIP

Foreword

For much of the first half of this century, American social science was actively engaged in overcoming what Walter Lippmann in 1922 identified as "the central difficulty of self-government" in the modern world, namely, the difficulty of creating a public competent to confront complexity and change without retreating into political passivity. Quantitative social scientists set out to devise ways of tracking and analyzing change that would make it comprehensible to the public. Social "reporting," as originally conceived, was integral to the underlying political purpose of social science: the accommodation of a plurality of interests in the context of expanding popular expectations.

The classic monument to this commitment was the two-volume *Recent Social Trends,* prepared by the President's Research Committee on Recent Social Trends and published in 1933. The blending of science and public information characteristic of the day is expressed in the summary of the committee's findings: "in the formulation of . . . new and emergent values, in the construction of the new symbols to thrill men's souls, in the contrivance of the new institutions and adaptations useful in the fulfillment of new aspirations, we trust that this review of recent social trends may prove of value to the American public."

Optimism about the role of empirical social science continued into the era of the Great Depression, although it came to emphasize the problems introduced by change rather than progressive improvements. This work nonetheless reflected engaged, hopeful concern, as did the contributions of American social scientists to the war effort that followed. When social science emerged from World War II, however, its characteristic posture was far more ironic than formerly, less confident in the meaning of its indicators, more hermetic, more specialized. The task of systematic description and analysis of recent social change fell further away from the ordinary activities of academic social scientists.

As editors of the series Social Trends in the United States, we contend that social science has a collective responsibility to report findings about society to the public, in order to contribute to the informed choices that are necessary in a democracy. If the reports of social scientists are to be useful to citizens, their authors must define questions for educational and political relevance and must translate technical terminology into the language of common discourse. Modern statistical methods make it possible to trace change along a large number of dimensions in which the pattern of change over time is rarely visible to people directly involved in it, and to discern how change in one dimension may affect change in others. Such information, in compact and comprehensible form, can make a useful contribution to political discussion.

This is the rationale of the series, which is sponsored by the Committee on Social Indicators of the Social Science Research Council. The committee invites authoritative scholars to contribute manuscripts on particular topics and has other scholars review each manuscript with attention to both the scientific and the broadly educational purposes of the series. Nevertheless, the volumes in the series are the authors' own, and thus far from uniform. Each is free-standing, but we hope that the effect of the series will be cumulative. Taken together, these volumes will not constitute an overall contemporary history: historical accounts evoke context rather than extract single dimensions of change. The series, however, will provide insights into interconnected aspects of contemporary society that no contemporary history— and no one interested in understanding our present condition— should ignore.

James A. Davis and John Modell

Contents

Religious Change in America

Chapter 1

Introduction

Religion has been with the human species at least since the time of early Neanderthal cave burials in what we now call the Middle East. It is, as someone has said, at minimum the modest doctrine that God is not mad.

Religion reassures humankind in both its moments of agony (seemingly without end) and its moments of ecstasy (all too brief) that there is some purpose in life beyond life itself, that the universe is something more than a concatenation of chance phenomena, that death does not have the final word to say about human life.

As best we know the history of the species, most humans have been religious: they have at least paid lip service to whatever deities have been assumed to preside over their universe and have listened with some willingness to believe to the stories of how those deities deal with humans, stories which are templates for interpreting and directing one's life.

Nonetheless, only a few humans in any of the eras about which we know much have been intensely devout during their whole lives. The gods and their rituals and their stories were available for special occasions. Other meaning systems directed daily life much of the time. If religion is the modest doctrine that God is not mad, religious devotion has been the modest attempt on the part of humans to hedge their bet against the apparent truth of that doctrine.

Dissent from the accepted faiths has perhaps not been so rare, although public dissent (à la Socrates) is rarely recorded. Until the Enlightenment, no one argued that humans did not need religion, much less that religion itself would wither away with the increase of scientific knowledge and the development of education. Since then, the conflict between science and religion has seemed inevitably destined to produce a victory for science. If scientific knowledge is the only valid form of human knowledge, then religion, which can make no claim to scientific method, can survive only as long as ignorance and superstition prevent humans from understanding science.

Moreover as technology, the offspring of science, gives humans more control over their world, the need to regard the world with religious awe will disappear. It is, as the German scripture scholar Rudolph Bultmann remarked, difficult to believe in the mystery of lightning when one can control electricity with the flick of a light switch.

Much social scientific work on religion starts with the assumption that humans are not as religious as they used to be and that any indicator of religious attitude or behavior ought therefore to show a decline in the importance of religion (although American scholars of the sociology of religion have generally in recent years come to question that assumption).

This book is a modest attempt to ask how well religion has in fact fared in the United States since 1940, when survey research began to ask questions about American religious attitudes and behavior.

We would think on first consideration of such questions that religion in America must have changed enormously since the time when the Great Depression was yielding to the Second World War. In 1940 most Americans did not own automobiles. Airplane travel was the privilege of the very few. Only a few suburbs clustered around the great cities. A substantial proportion of the population still lived on farms. Television was still an experimental phenomenon. Birthrates had fallen during the Great Depression, divorce rates were still very low, and, outside certain elite groups, divorce was viewed as a disgrace. There were only half as many Americans as there are today, and one dollar could buy goods and services which require almost eight dollars today. The income of Americans in constant dollars (adjusted for inflation) was only one-quarter what it is in the 1980s.

How can a society, it might well be asked, endure such changes in the space of little less than half a century and not have its religious beliefs and behaviors shaken to their foundations? Surely Americans are not as religious as they were in the small towns and urban neighborhoods of the late 1930s—are they? American religion must have changed, it will be argued; the only question is of what sort the change might be.

Three incidents out of many exemplify this attitude. In the autumn of 1984 a weekly newsmagazine reported that, despite the influence of the Moral Majority, religion was on the wane in the United States: the most recent Gallup poll on church attendance showed that it was not increasing at as rapid a rate as it had in previous years. That winter, the anchorman on a national evening newscast informed viewers that the just-published *Statistical Abstract of the United States* showed that Americans were not attending church services as much as they had in the past. Finally, when the Social Science Research Council (SSRC) invited me to prepare this book, its letter assumed that one of the major tasks of a study of religious indicators over the past half-century would be to document the "secularization" of the American population—the decline, in other words, of religious commitment in American life.

There are two sorts of vested interests in the alleged decline of religion. Those who themselves are not religious—frequently having broken with the religious affiliations and practices of their childhood—find, in what seems to them to be the decline of religious commitment and devotion, proof that their own decision was the correct one, a mere anticipation of where everyone else is headed. On the other hand are those religious leaders who use the alleged decline of faith as a tool to cajole their followers to return, after suitable penance and conversion, to a golden age of piety and devotion. Both groups would even agree on the reasons for the decline of religion—secularism, materialism, science, the lure of hedonism, the restlessness of youth. The difference between the unbeliever and the leader of believers is that the former sees the process of decline as irreversible, whereas the latter thinks that the decline can be turned around, though with difficulty, by a revival of religious fervor—either, if the leader is of the liberal persuasion, by dedication to "justice and peace" or, if the leader is of a conservative or fundamentalist persuasion, by dedication to the traditional principles and practices of the religious heritage.

As will be seen in the following chapters, none of the models of religious decline implicit in the three anecdotes above satisfactorily fits the data that are available to those who study American religion empirically. The reason for presenting these models in narrative form at the outset is to illustrate the powerful assumptions about religion which exist in elite segments of American society. Those who challenge such assumptions must exercise considerable rigor in their data analysis and presentation if they expect to obtain a hearing.

Religion, in other words, like politics, taxes, sex, and word-processing programs, is a topic about which there are strong feelings, predispositions, convictions. Any attempt to pull together the available data about religious attitudes and behaviors for the last half-century must therefore be based both on rigorous assumptions and on clearly defined limits. I am not essaying here a study of American religion but merely, and much more modestly, a report on the changes in American religion in the years since national surveys began; and, rather than attempting to tell the "whole story" of American religion since the Great Depression, I am limiting myself, by assignment and training, to the part of the story which can be gleaned from survey data. Moreover, I begin with the fundamental assumption that it is better to use data about which there are the fewest possible doubts, at the cost of a more schematic story, than to use more dubious data to tell a richer and more interesting story. I therefore hold myself to three rules:

1. I use only indicators that are represented by questions asked over time. If a question was asked in a survey only in the last five years, for example, I resist the temptation of the good-old-days fallacy (or bad old days, depending upon one's perspective) to suggest that, "Well, we all know that such a striking attitude or behavior didn't exist forty years ago." I am prepared to make judgments about what happened forty years ago only if I have the same indicator from a survey then. Other evidence about, say, the frequency of intense religious experience in the 1940s may be useful and interesting in a historical monograph about religious experience, but it has no place in a social indicators report.

2. I insist that the wording of the question be the same throughout the period in which it was used. A modified indicator is a new indicator—unless there is a link which connects the two (no such links exist, as far as I am aware, in religious indicators).

3. Finally, I use only data from "multistage" or "strict probability" national samples, in which each unit in the population has an equal chance of being chosen. As useful as studies of the San Francisco Bay area or the Detroit area may be, they are not national studies. They provide excellent information on those two interesting areas of the country—which have the good fortune of being adjacent to universities with survey research competence—but neither the Bay nor Detroit is America. One cannot and should not generalize from changes which may or may not have occurred in these locales to the rest of the country—not, at any rate, in a study of national social indicators.

At the end, therefore, I will be content to say, "This is at least what we know about American religion since 1940, and know with considerable confidence from the survey data."

In general, there are five models to be tested against the survey data available to us:

1. *The secularization model.* In this perspective, perhaps the most common among social scientists, it is assumed that religion is—perhaps necessarily and self-evidently—on the wane in the Western urbanized, industrialized nations. Perhaps there are occasional "blips" in the trajectories, but science, technology, universal education and the demystification or—to use the theologian's term—"demythologization" of the cosmos represent separately and together forces of irreligion which the traditional faiths cannot endure over the long run. Science will inevitably win its long-standing conflict with religion.

2. *The cyclic model.* Other observers note that religion in the United States seems to persist doggedly long after it ought to have disappeared. To them there seem to be ebbs and flows in religion, great cyclic movements of rise and fall, of secularization and, to use a word of which Peter Berger is fond, "resacralization." Perhaps the long-term trajectories are still down, but religion has remarkable residual power to reassert its hold on human beings, particularly in conservative political times. Those who embrace this model might argue that in the period 1940–1985 there were swings of the giant pendulum in favor of religion in the 1950s and the 1980s—times of patriotism and conservative Republican presidencies—the decades of Dwight Eisenhower and Ronald Reagan.

3. *The episodic event model.* In this perspective, religious changes may be the result of "one-shot" events which have an impact but are not repeated. Thus some observers of the American family contend that the increase in divorces in the 1970s and the subsequent end of this increase were the result of a " trauma" to the existing system caused by the invention of the birth control pill, the greater control it gave women over their own fertility, and the resultant greater freedom to pursue economic independence through entry into the work force. Once this change had been "absorbed," these observers suggest, the trajectory of family dissolution rates leveled off. During the years under consideration in this book, the Second Vatican Council mandated substantial

changes in the Catholic church. This could be an episodic event which had considerable impact on the religious behavior of American Catholics. Whether that impact was in fact long-term or episodic remains to be tested against the data.

4. *The stability model.* While change is news, the absence of change is not. Yet many aspects of the human condition do not change—conflict between faculty and administration, eventual marriage of most humans, intergenerational conflict. Because of its profound importance as the "ultimate symbol system," the system of answers to the most fundamental questions of meaning about which the human person can wonder, religion is one of those relatively immutable dimensions of human behavior which will not change much over time, at least not in the short run (say, two decades) or the medium run (a half-century, more or less).

5. *The religious growth model.* Although no one that I know of has seriously proposed that there is a propensity for humankind to grow more religious (perhaps in the face of the seemingly permanent threat of nuclear annihilation), for reasons of logic it should be considered as a possibility to be tested. The trajectories might well be headed up instead of down.

The first two models have the greatest appeal because of their symmetry and elegance. Great sweeping movements which can be used to order and explain much that puzzles us in the human condition are more attractive than episodic accidents or the monotony of a phenomenon that changes very little, if at all. Yet elegance and symmetry, as useful as they are for preliminary consideration of phenomena, are not finally decisive. The question to which a serious analysis must address itself is whether, in addition to being elegant, a model also fits the data.

There is nothing inherently contradictory about the five models presented above. They all might be true of different parts of the elephant of American religious behavior. And indeed, it is possible that at the end of this investigation, we might be reduced to observing, in effect, that some indicators are going up, some are going down, some are remaining stable, some have been jolted by various one-shot traumas, and some seem subject to periodic cycles that are not unlike the business cycles—unquestionable, but mostly inexplicable.

In fact there are some data which fit each of the five models. Certainly the stability model, with some minor modifications to improve the goodness of fit, cannot be rejected: the indicators show much more stability than change in American religion. Religion may be in decline in the United States, but that decline cannot be proved from the available social indicator data.

The ordinary strategy of social research is to seek differences and then to attempt to explain the differences. In this book the differences to be sought are changes over time in religious behavior. Where there are no changes, there are no differences to explain. Stability, then, needs no explanation, but change does. One result of this strategy is that there is more analysis of Catholics in the following chapters than of Protestants, because most of the observable changes in religious indicators are limited to the Catholic population. Protestants' religious attitudes and behavior have not changed greatly in the last half century. Catholics' religious attitudes and behavior have, as has their social and economic condition. However, the former does not seem to be the result of the latter.

There are several special difficulties in the study of religious social indicators.

1. There simply are not as many indicators of religion as there are of race or family life. Accordingly, an analysis of American religion must necessarily be less elaborate than one of American racial or familial or occupational attitudes and behavior. Given only a handful of religious items that go back to the beginning of surveys (one as far back as 1939), we are constrained to paint a very sketchy picture of American religion before the 1960s.

2. Although all three major sources of our data—the Gallup organization (AIPO; American Institute of Public Opinion), the Survey Research Center of the University of Michigan (SRC), and

NORC (formerly the National Opinion Research Center) at the University of Chicago—provide high-quality data, intensive analysis of the relationship between religion and other variables became practical only with the institution of the annual NORC General Social Survey (GSS). The GSS has been administered every year but two since 1972 to some 1,500 respondents. Some questions are asked every year, some every other year, some every three years. Thus the number of cases for most questions in the survey runs from 7,000 to more than 20,000. As a result we can speak with greater confidence of American religion from the early 1970s to the present than we can of previous years. In order to provide enough cases for statistical confidence, in the following chapters I will often cluster the twelve General Social Surveys into three groups: "early 1970s" (1972–1975), "late 1970s" (1976–1980), and "early 1980s" (1982–1985 or –1986). (There was no GSS in 1979 and 1981.) (One of the most important early studies of American religion was done in 1952 for the *Catholic Digest* by Ben Gaffin Associates. Unfortunately, the data cards from that study have been lost; thus it is impossible to analyze any change from that base point to subsequent research.)

3. The limited size of national samples makes it virtually impossible to discuss change in smaller denominations. "What about Mormons?" or "What about the Unitarians?" are the sorts of questions I am frequently asked after lectures on these subjects. I have to reply that there are not enough respondents in the ordinary survey to talk confidently even about Jews, much less about smaller groups. Since Jews make up approximately 3 percent of the American population, a typical survey of 1,500 respondents will include only between 40 and 50 whose denominational affiliation is Jewish. Even combining five years of GSSs will provide only a few more than 200 Jewish respondents. No responsible scholar would attempt serious analysis of religious behavior with such inadequate numbers. In fact, with the data resources now available, we can confidently address only two broad categories: "Protestant" and "'Catholic." Within the

Protestant category, it is possible to break out two large denominations—Methodists and Baptists—for detailed change analysis, should this seem to be necessary. (Catholics are approximately one-quarter of the American population, Baptists about one-fifth, Methodists about one-sixth.) Fortunately, the trends to be reported here will rarely require us to consider smaller denominations. However, it does not follow that their own development and history are not important or different. It follows only that what is happening to them does not affect the "big picture" of American religion which is the concern of this book.

4. Although many scholars, most notably Clifford Geertz, are persuaded that religion is a "symbol system" which provides meaning and direction in the face of life's ultimate questions, and that hence religious symbols, pictures, and images are likely to have a greater impact on human behavior than are doctrinal propositions and devotional practices, there are no social indicators which can be used to measure changes (if any) in these symbol systems. In Chapter 9 I suggest some survey items already in use which may make possible a future study of changes in the religious imagination.

5. Religion correlates with age. In any given survey, older people are more likely to be religious than younger people. When a youthful cohort is especially large, it will depress the average in religious devotion measures even though no actual change is necessarily occurring in the age-specific rates. As we shall see, the large youthful cohort did contribute by its sheer size to the decline in Catholic church attendance in the late 1960s and the early 1970s. However, in addition to the population distribution (more young people who are less religious) there was also a decline that was spread evenly throughout all Catholic age cohorts. Thus there was both a population distribution decline and an actual decline at all age levels.

A correlation between religion and age observed at a given time may be either a life-cycle or cohort phenomenon. If younger people are less religious merely because they are young but will become more religious as they grow older, then the phenomenon observed is a life-cycle event and indicates no long-term religious trend toward secularization (religious decline). However, if the young are less religious and will remain so as they age, then we are observing a cohort phenomenon—the emergence of a permanently less religious group which may indicate a secular (long- or medium-term) trend. Thus we must ask whether the young people who matured during the 1960s are less religious now because they are young, because they grew up in troubled times, or because they represent the beginning or continuation of a decline in religious devotion.

By complex statistical analysis it is sometimes possible to separate the impact of cohort from that of life cycle. In effect, the process is not unlike that by which computer-driven scanners enhance the signals sent by space vehicles to produce pictures of the object photographed which best fit the data being received. We must ask, for example, how the numbers in a table would be distributed if there was only a life-cycle effect on religious behavior and no cohort effect. Then we compare this distribution of numbers with the actual distribution of cases in the sample to see if the former is different at a level of statistical significance from the latter. If there is a difference, then cohort must be taken into account in explaining the data. If there is not a significant difference, then we conclude that a model which contains a life-cycle effect on religious behavior, but no cohort effect, cannot be rejected.

There are three broad categories of chapters in the remainder of this book. Chapters 2 through 6 focus on religion as a dependent variable; Chapters 7 and 8 treat religion as an independent variable and examine its effect on other forms of attitude and behavior—economic and political. Finally, Chapter 9 suggests a new set of religious indicators which might be useful additions to some future study; unlike the measures analyzed in this book, they are able to explain other forms of human behavior.

Given the widespread presumption in favor of the secularization model, I propose as the guiding null hypothesis (the hypothesis that can most safely be rejected in the face of the data) that there is no major decline in American religious faith and devotion cannot be rejected. My investigation of the data will then require that I first attempt to falsify that hypothesis, to prove that there is a notable, even a statistically significant, decline in American religion.

That assignment turns out to be a difficult one indeed.

Chapter 2

Religious Doctrine

There are time-series data (responses to the same question asked at different points in time) to test four of the five models described in the previous chapter in relation to religious belief. Most of the belief items demonstrate not mutability but remarkable durability over time. Whatever else may have happened in American religion, the central doctrinal beliefs of Americans have not changed in the forty years during which survey questions have been asked about these beliefs.

Thus AIPO data show that more than nine out of ten Americans have believed in the existence of God in every survey since 1944—97 percent in 1944 and 95 percent in 1981 (see Table 2.1A). During the same span of time, the divinity of Jesus has been accepted by a little more than three-fourths of those surveyed—77 percent in 1952 and 76 percent in 1983 (Table 2.1B). The positive response—those believing in the divinity of Jesus—combines "God" and "Son of God" responses, the latter being 3 percent in 1952 and 1965 and 6 percent in 1983.

Americans also are convinced that God is important in their lives. AIPO (1985) reports that on a 10-point scale rating the importance of God, Americans score 8.2; in Ireland the score is 8.0, in Italy 6.9, in Spain 6.4, in Britain and Germany 5.7, and in Sweden 3.9. There are no data from the past on responses to this question.

In more recent years AIPO has asked once about the resurrection of Jesus and once explicitly about the divinity of Jesus. On

Table 2.1.   Religious beliefs

	Year	%
A. Do you believe in the existence of God or a universal spirit?		
	1944	97
	1954	96
	1967	97
	1981	95
B. Do you believe that Jesus Christ ever actually lived? Do you think He was God or just another leader like Mohammed or Buddha?		
	1952	77
	1965	75
	1983	76
C. Do you believe there is a life after death?		
	1944	76
	1952	77
	1965	75
	1975	76
	1985	74
D. Do you think there is a heaven where people who have led good lives are eternally rewarded?		
	1952	72
	1965	68
	1980	71
E. Do you believe there is a hell?		
	1952	58
	1965	54
	1980	53

Sources: 1975 and 1985: GSS. All other years: AIPO, 1985.

the first item, which asked respondents how certain they were on a scale of 1 to 10 about the Resurrection, 65 percent rated themselves at 10 and another 11 percent at 8 or 9. On the second item, which asked how respondents felt about the statement "I believe in the divinity of Jesus Christ," 60 percent said that they felt the statement was "completely true" and another 25 percent said that it was "mostly true." Although neither item is a time series, both provide an indication of Americans' (continuing?) orthodoxy.

Nor is any change to be found in belief in an afterlife. From 1944 to 1985, in the most recent GSS, approximately three-quarters of Americans have believed in life after death (Table 2.1C). During the same period some 6 or 7 percent of respondents have been uncertain about the matter, and one-fifth have consistently rejected the idea of an afterlife. Moreover, it appears that most of those who do believe in life after death also believe in heaven—72 percent of Americans in 1952 and 71 percent in 1980 (Table 2.1D). There has, however, been a decline in belief in hell—from 58 percent in 1952 to 53 percent in 1980 (Table 2.1E). (No analysis of this 5 percent decline is possible because the 1952 data, from the Ben Gaffin *Catholic Digest* study, were lost. However, the decline over twenty-eight years may very well be an age-related phenomenon, since the population has a larger proportion of young people now than it did then.)

What do Americans think heaven is like? Although there are no data from the past, recent GSS surveys reveal that 82 percent imagine it as "very likely" to be a union with God, 68 percent picture it as a life of peace and tranquillity and union with loved ones, only 5 percent expect it to be a pale shadowy life, and 20 percent think it will lack many of the things which make our present life enjoyable. A third, on the other hand, believe that life after death will be a paradise of pleasures and delights. We have no way of knowing how these images have changed, if at all, in the last fifty years.

Belief in life after death is not only invariant over time; it is also not affected by such variables as age or education. In both 1944 and 1985 college-educated young people (under thirty) and grammar-school-educated older people (over sixty) were equally committed to the proposition that there is life after death. Only in Ireland is belief in life after death as strong as it is in the United States (AIPO, 1985, p. 53), followed by Spain, Finland, and Italy, where about half the respondents believe in it; then, close behind, Great Britain, Norway, and the Netherlands, where more than two-fifths accept life after death. In West Germany, Belgium, and France the belief is to be found in a little more than a third of the respondents, and in Denmark in approximately a quarter. This persistence of an orthodox belief in an afterlife by the Western world's best-educated and most modernized population, in contrast to a decline in many other Western countries, has not been satisfactorily explained by social science. The final chapter offers some speculations which, for the present, are nothing more than educated guesses.

There has been, however, a decline in Americans' acceptance of the literal truth of the Bible. The nature of this decline is obscured by the unsatisfactory wording of the AIPO question:

Which one of these statements comes closest to describing your feelings about the Bible:

The Bible is a collection of writings representing some of the religious philosophies of ancient man.

The Bible is the word of God but is sometimes mistaken in its statements and teachings.

The Bible is the word of God and is not mistaken in its statements and teachings.

The difficulty lies in the second and third responses, in which statements and teachings are lumped together. A moderate literalism would see the fundamental teachings of the Bible as unmistaken but its obiter dicta—such as the famous Red Sea passage about the sun revolving around the earth, which caused Galileo so much trouble—as frequently mistaken. The choices offered by SRC seem to take that distinction into account:

The Bible is God's word and all it says is true.

The Bible was written by men inspired by God, but it contains some human errors.

The Bible is a good book because it was written by wise men but God had nothing to do with it.

The Bible was written by men who lived so long ago that it is worth very little today.

On both items there has been a decline in the strictest form of literalism, the sharpest falloff being between 1963 and 1968 in the AIPO question, from 65 percent to 38 percent (Table 2.2A). There has also been a decline in the SRC question, which has been used frequently by NORC and is now included in the GSS. When the first two responses are combined, in the 1985 GSS, more than nine of every ten respondents subscribed to at least moderate literalism.

However, there has been a decline in the SRC/GSS item of the acceptance of the strictest interpretation of biblical inerrancy on which some denominational traditions might insist: between 1968 and 1985 it fell from 53 percent to 45 percent.

As Figure 2.1 shows, the greatest decline in the strictest form

Table 2.2.   Biblical attitudes and practices (%)

A. *Belief in the literal truth of the Bible*

Year	AIPO question	NORC/SRC question
1963–64	65	48
1968–69	38	53
1984–85	38	45

B. *Bible readership*

Year	Read daily
1942	10
1965	14
1984	15

C. *Knowledge of the Bible*

Year	Know who delivered Sermon on the Mount	Can name all 4 Gospels	Know where Jesus was born
1954	34	35	64
1982	42	46	70

Sources: NORC/SRC data from analysis of GSS, 1985. All other data from AIPO, 1985.

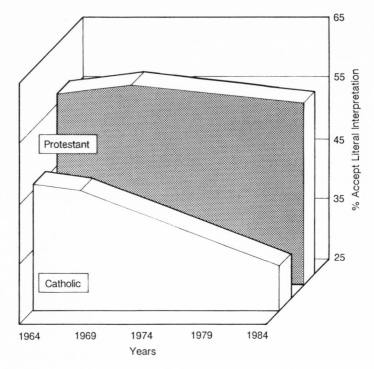

Figure 2.1. Literal interpretation of Bible among Catholics and Protestants, 1964–1984 (SRC, 1964, 1968; NORC, 1985).

of biblical literalism has occurred among those whose religious teaching does not hold them to strict literalism—Catholics. A model which asserts that the decline in acceptance of strict literalism has occurred only among younger (under-thirty) and better-educated (college-attending) Catholics, and especially among those who are both younger and better educated, cannot be rejected. Perhaps as a result of the clarification of Catholic scriptural doctrine in the famous constitution *Dei Verbum* of the Second Vatican Council, Catholics, and especially the younger and better educated, and even more especially those who are both young and better educated, have modified their position on biblical literalism. This change accounts entirely for the lower rates of acceptance of literalism in American respondents during the last twenty years (on the SRC/GSS measure). What seems to be a decline (secularization model) turns out to be in all probability the result of an "episodic event" which did not move those affected by it to a position which was for them any less orthodox (and is, as a matter of fact, more orthodox).

The other story presented in Figure 2.1—continued Protestant acceptance of the strict literal interpretation of the Bible—calls into question the accuracy of the many media reports on the rise of fundamentalism in the last decade. Nothing could be more "fundamentalistic" than belief in strict literal interpretation of the Bible. Yet there has been no increase in the proportion of Protestants holding that conviction: the proportion was a little more than half twenty-five years ago and remains unchanged today.

Bible reading and biblical knowledge have actually increased modestly in the last several decades (Table 2.2B,C). Yet such an increase (from 10 percent to 15 percent) in the daily reading of the Bible is hardly enough to account for the claim of a fundamentalist or evangelist revival in recent years. AIPO has collected data since 1976 on three items which may fairly be said to constitute a scale of fundamentalist/evangelist orientation: the experience of being "born again," a literalist view of the Bible, and a report of an attempt to encourage someone else to accept Jesus Christ as savior. The born-again experience has increased from 36 to 40 percent, literalism has decreased only from 38 to 37 percent, and encouraging someone to accept Jesus has likewise decreased only from 48 to 47 percent. In 1976 18 percent of respondents gave positive responses to all three items; in 1984, this figure had risen to 22 percent. These changes, both in individual items and in the scale of all three items, do not yet represent either an impressive religious movement or even a statistically significant change.

The fundamentalist/evangelical segment of American religious groups composes at least one-fifth of the American population.

Perhaps the so-called revival is nothing more than journalists' discovery of a phenomenon which historians and sociologists of American religion have always known was present and important. Like belief in God and in life after death, this component of American religion seems to be neither decreasing nor increasing. The stability model, in other words, fits the AIPO data about fundamentalism better than any of the others.

The only decline in American religious convictions that can be documented with certainty is American Catholics' acceptance of papal authority. In 1963 (NORC) 70 percent of American Catholics believed as "certainly true" that Jesus had handed over authority in the church to Peter and his successors, the popes; 68 percent believed with certainty that in some matters the pope was infallible (Greeley, McCready, and McCourt, 1976; Greeley and Rossi, 1965). In 1974 these percentages had declined to 42 and 32 percent, respectively, and in 1980, in a study of Catholics under thirty, to 20 percent.

Thus an investigation of the social indicators of American doctrinal convictions shows that there has been both stability and decline—with an occasional increase in such practices as daily Bible reading which reveal doctrinal convictions. The stability seems to have been Protestant, the decline Catholic. In the latter case it is not unreasonable to assume that the decline in belief in the inerrancy of the Bible to a position which is still orthodox, if not more orthodox, is the result of the clarification of this matter at the Second Vatican Council. As we shall see, the change in attitudes on authority seems to be linked to another major Catholic event of the 1960s, the birth control encyclical *Humanae Vitae.*

Chapter 3

Denominations

The United States is a denominational society, as Will Herberg (1960) contended in his classic study of thirty years ago. Herberg meant not merely that unlike England, with its established Protestant church, or Italy, which is an entirely Catholic society, the United States is composed of many different denominations under the general rubric of Protestants, Catholics, and Jews. He also meant that denominational affiliation tends to be an important part of Americans' self-definition and social location. When asked by neighbors what they are, an American family, moving into a new house, more or less automatically tends to reply that they are "Protestant," "Catholic" or "Jewish." Under some circumstances, an ethnic identification may be added to "Catholic" or a more specific denominational affiliation to the generic "Protestant," or "Jewish."

Within this context of religious identification, Wade Clark Roof and William McKinney (1987) in an excellent monograph suggest that there are three dynamics at work: the flow from conservative to liberal churches, the flow from liberal to conservative churches, and the flow out of the churches to secularity. In principle it ought to be easy to measure these flows and to determine whether religious affiliation is holding its own and in particular whether traditional denominations are sustaining themselves against the onslaughts of humanism.

However, four factors complicate any such analysis:

1. Denominational statistics compiled by the churches them-

selves are of little help, both because the quality control in such data collection is problematic (Catholic pastor filling out report for the *Official Catholic Directory*, to associate pastor: "How many families do we have?" Associate in reply: "Oh, about two thousand, I think.") and because the criteria for membership differ along denominational lines: Catholics claim everyone who has been baptized Catholic (but are vague about who these people may be); mainline Protestants—Methodists, Lutherans, Episcopalians, and Presbyterians—tend to have rigorous criteria; evangelicals and fundamentalists tend to make enthusiastic claims.

2. Survey statistics, which ought to solve problem 1, are contradictory: the Gallup Organization reports a drastic decline in Protestant membership over the last half-century and an equally dramatic increase in Catholic affiliation, but other survey organizations do not record the same change.

3. Even if it were possible to determine with some confidence what changes there are in the distribution among religious denominations (should there be such changes), it would be difficult to explain the changes without knowing which members of a denomination have left to join another denomination. For example, there appears to have been a sharp decline in the proportion of Americans who identify as Methodists. But unless we know which members of other denominations have once been Methodist we can only speculate on the reasons for their change. The General Social Survey is a useful tool for addressing this problem because for most of its years it has asked not only about current denomination but also about the denomination in which the respondent was raised.

4. Because of the baby boom (roughly 1945–1960) the adult American population has a far larger proportion of young people than it did thirty years ago. Religious behavior characteristic of young people will therefore increase in the population, but this does not necessarily mean that there will have been a change in religion—unless it can be established that young people continue in this behavior as they grow older. Another example of a life-

cycle effect is that crime rates increase when the population is disproportionately youthful; but it follows that there is a real change in the culture of the country only if a greater proportion of people in their twenties and thirties are criminal than were people of the same ages in the past.

The social science category most useful for analyzing this issue is the cohort, the group of people born in a given set of years. By walking a number of cohorts through the various stages of their life cycle and comparing, say, those born in the 1940s with those born in the 1950s when they were the same age, we can determine whether there is real cultural change taking place or whether what looks like cultural change is in fact merely the result of a larger number of young people in the population. The General Social Survey is extremely useful for such analysis because it walks age groups through the last fifteen years of American history.

There is an increase in the number of Americans who have no religious identification (although that increase seems to have stopped in the mid-1970s) (Glenn, 1987). Does this mean that there is in fact an increase in "secularity" among Americans, or is it merely the result of the fact that there are more younger people in the population and it takes young people a while to make up their minds about denominational affiliation?

Most European sociologists who study religion and many Americans too assume that an age correlation with religious behavior indicates that there has been a decline in religious practice and that this decline is likely to continue. But such an assumption is valid only if one can prove that a greater proportion of the young people in their twenties today are not, for example, affiliated with a denomination than, say, twenty years ago. One must do repeated surveys or at least have surveys taken at different times to answer such a question; any effort to argue from age correlation to social change on the basis of a single survey is risky, not to say dishonest.

Moreover, it is obvious from work in other branches of sociology that the teenage and young-adult years are a time of exploration preparatory to definitive identification. The young are less likely than their elders to have made decisions about occupation, career, residence, political affiliation, permanent sexual partner. But as time goes on, they do indeed make these decisions—they affiliate with a profession, a career, a community, a party, a spouse. To assume on a priori grounds that the same processes are not at work in the religious dimension of life is absurd.

In short, age correlations without cohort analysis prove nothing.

The first denominational issue we must address is the difference among the various national survey organizations in the distribution of the population among religious groups. AIPO reports major changes over the years. Other survey groups find no change or only slight changes.

According to a table on denominational affiliations in the 1982 edition of *Religion in America* (AIPO, 1982), between 1947 and 1981 the proportion of American Catholics rose from 20 percent to 28 percent, the proportion of Protestants fell from 69 to 59 percent, and the proportion of Jews fell from 5 percent to 2 percent. According to the table this represents a 40 percent increase for Catholics, a 15 percent decline for Protestants, and a 60 percent decline for Jews. In 1985 AIPO reported a Protestant decline to 57 percent (Table 3.1). According to the 1985 table the changes had occurred since the late 1960s and affected especially Methodists and Presbyterians, who together have lost since 1967 9 percentage points of their 1967 20 percent of Americans, either to Catholics or to "other"—presumably more fundamentalist—Protestants. Such a dramatic transformation in the shape of American religious pluralism would be striking indeed and presumably should have been headline news, as was the slight 1985 decline in Catholic affiliation as reported by the *Official Catholic Directory*.

In the logic of social science, a striking finding can be tested

Table 3.1. American religious groups, 1947–1985 (%)

Year	Protestant	Catholic	Jewish	Other	None
AIPO					
1947	69	20	5	1	6
1957	66	26	3	1	2
1962	70	23	3	2	2
1967	67	25	3	2	2
1972	63	26	2	4	5
1980	60	29	2	1	6
1985	57	28	2	4	9
NORC/GSS					
1963	67	24	2	4	2
1967	66	24	2	3	5
1972	65	25	3	1	6
1977	65	25	2	1	7
1985	65	25	2	1	7
SRC					
1952–60	73	21	3	1	2
1964–72	71	22	2	1	3
1976–80	64	24	3	2	7

Sources: AIPO, 1985; pooled amalgam samples, NORC, 1963 and 1967, GSS, 1972, 1977, 1985; pooled presidential election years, SRC.

Note: AIPO and NORC ask about "religious preference." Before the 1970s SRC asked: "What is your religious preference: Protestant, Catholic, or Jewish?" Since then it has added: "or something else?"

only by replication. Do other survey data sets confirm the apparent erosion of Protestantism and Judaism?

It is extremely difficult to replicate the AIPO findings. For the last twenty years NORC has consistently found that 25 percent of its respondents were Catholic (Table 3.1). In the first national Catholic study in 1963 (Greeley and Rossi, 1965) my colleague Peter H. Rossi and I reported that 25 percent of Americans were Catholic at a time when AIPO data indicated that they were 23 percent of the population. In two studies in 1972 and 1974, NORC researchers also found 25 percent of respondents to be Catholic, and this figure has remained constant through the twelve General Social Surveys. In other words, the apparent increase in the Catholic proportion of Americans since 1962, reported by AIPO, simply is not to be observed in NORC data for the same period.

What are we to make of the contrasting AIPO and NORC reports of American denominationalism during the last several decades? First, it should be noted that the NORC findings represent data from three different sample frames, each based on a decennial census. Thus the consistency of Catholic proportions has already been replicated twice by NORC. Moreover, there is nothing in the convert data reported in the *Official Catholic Directory* to confirm a 25 percent increase in Catholics (from 23 to 29 percent) in the last twenty years. Although the statistics in the *Directory* are devoid of quality control, in a crude way they can be trusted on the matter of converts, if only because a pastor can check the number of converts in his parish merely by glancing at his baptismal records for the past year—a much easier task than estimating the number of people in his parish. Moreover, since the diocesan tax is normally based on the size of a parish, the tax is not increased by the addition of converts, unless there is an enormous number of them in a given year.

Thus the AIPO data must be treated with great caution. The redistribution of denominationalism implied in these data is not replicated and must therefore be considered not proved. Perhaps it is the result of a modification of AIPO sampling techniques.

SRC election surveys produce yet a third pattern (Table 3.1). Since the early 1960s SRC notes a 9 percentage point decline in Protestant affiliation and a 3 percentage point increase in Catholic affiliation. However, in the 1970s, SRC changed its question from "What is your religious affiliation: Protestant, Catholic, or Jewish?" to "What is your religious affiliation: Protestant, Catholic, Jewish, or something else?"

Thus AIPO shows a 13 percentage point decline in Protestant affiliation since the early 1960s, SRC a 7 percentage point decline, and NORC a 2 percentage point decline. AIPO reports a 5 percent increase for Catholics, SRC a 2 percent increase, and NORC no change.

The AIPO account seems to be inaccurate because it disagrees with the combined reports of the two academic centers. In choosing between SRC and NORC, we must keep two facts in mind: (1) NORC has not changed the wording in its question, and (2) both groups agree about the current distribution of American denominational affiliation. Either NORC underestimated the proportion of Protestants in the early 1960s or SRC overestimated the proportion.

Finally, the sharp decline in the combined proportion of Methodists and Presbyterians reported by AIPO, from 20 percent to 11 percent in the period 1974–1984, is not replicated in GSS, which covers the same years. In 1975 these two denominations together represented 18 percent of Americans, in 1985 16 percent. Presbyterians had suffered no decline at all, and the Methodist loss (to "others") was 3 percentage points. There has been a statistically significant decline in Methodist affiliation, but it is not of the magnitude reported by AIPO (Table 3.2). The Jewish decline, from 2.7 percent to 2.2 percent, is not statistically significant. Thus the only trace of replication of the AIPO findings

Table 3.2.   Protestant denominations, 1974–1985 (%)

Year	Baptist	Methodist	Lutheran	Presbyterian	Episcopalian	Other	None
AIPO							
1974	21	14	7	6	3	—	—
1978	19	11	6	4	2	—	—
1984	20	9	7	2	3	—	—
GSS							
1975	20	13	8	5	3	12	3
1980	20	12	8	5	3	13	3
1985	21	11	8	5	3	14	3

Sources: AIPO, 1985; pooled GSS: 1975 = 1972–1975, 1980 = 1976–1980, 1985 = 1981–1985.

in GSS is a decline in Methodist affiliation and one that was not nearly as sharp as AIPO had reported. Moreover, this loss produced no gain for Catholicism but rather an increase in "other" Protestants.

A final approach to the issue of the changing size of American denominations is made possible by a GSS question about respondents' religious affiliation when they were growing up: "In what religion were you raised?" The marginal distributions presented in Table 3.3 indicate rather little change. Indeed a model which asserts that the only statistically significant change is an increase (from 3 percent to 7 percent) of those with no religious affiliation cannot be rejected. The so-called mainline Protestant denominations show a combined loss of 3 percentage points, but the Baptists, who might be considered a more fundamentalist denomination, also lose 3 percentage points.

Two issues need to be considered in greater detail: the apparent increase in those with "no" religious affiliation and the apparent decrease in the mainline segment of Protestants.

Even in the NORC data the number of those with "no" religious affiliation has doubled since the early 1960s. There is

Table 3.3.   Present religion and religion in which one was raised, 1974–1987 (%)

Religion	Raised	Present	Difference
Baptist	24	21	− 3
Methodist	14	12	− 2
Lutheran	8	8	—
Presbyterian	5	4	− 1
Episcopalian	3	3	—
Other Protestant	11	13	2
Catholic	27	25	− 2
Jewish	3	2	− 1
None	3	7	4
Other	2	3	1

Sources: Pooled data, GSS, 1974–1987.

certainly (Figure 3.1) a strong correlation between no religious affiliation and age. Twelve percent of those in their twenties have no affiliation, in contrast to 3 percent of those over fifty. But is this correlation the result of aging, or is it the result of the fact that younger age cohorts are more likely to be unaffiliated, even granting their youthfulness, and hence will continue to be less affiliated through their life cycle?

There are, as is usual in such matters, three possible explanations: a long-run trend, a change that is limited to certain age cohorts, or a life-cycle phenomenon. In the first case the trend should continue as each new age group produces a larger share of religiously unaffiliated people. In the second case, certain cohorts would represent a "blip" in the continuing process of religious socialization. In the final case, the phenomenon would be

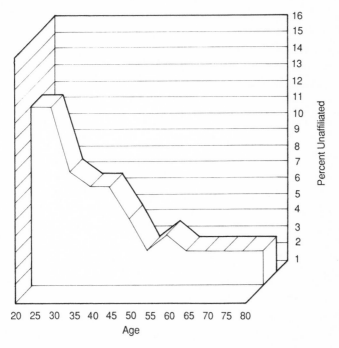

Figure 3.1. Population with no religious affiliation, by age (GSS, 1972–1987).

accounted for by the fact that younger people are less likely to be affiliated religiously but acquire religious affiliation as they grow older.

The first explanation is apparently disproved by the fact that there has been no significant increase in the proportion of unaffiliated during the fifteen years of the General Social Survey. In a choice between the latter two explanations, we are forced to favor the second by the fact that in a regression equation in which cohort and age are entered with the dependent variable being absence of religious affiliation, the standardized beta correlation with age is .13 and with cohort .02. (A beta correlation is the relationship between two variables taking into account the influence of all the other variables in the equation. In this case it means that, net of cohort, the correlation between no religious affiliation and age is .13, and, net of age, the relation between no affiliation and cohort is .02.)

Figure 3.2 illustrates this phenomenon by walking two synthetic cohorts through the life cycle from early twenties to early fifties. The first line, drawn from Figure 3.1, represents the path of a cohort if there is a significant relationship between age and no religious affiliation but no significant cohort relationship. To the extent that a given cohort follows this path, its pilgrimage away from and back to religion is purely a life-cycle phenomenon and represents no departure from the path of leaving religious affiliation when young and then reclaiming affiliation as it ages.

The other two lines are synthetic cohorts, because even in the General Social Survey there is not yet an actual cohort which has moved from its early twenties to its early fifties. The first synthetic cohort is a combination of the four cohorts (in five-year groupings) born between 1935 and 1950. The second consists of only the 1935 and 1950 cohorts. These two birth groups overlap only in their early thirties in the GSS (and at 8 percent unaffiliated for both).

The curve for nonaffiliation of the two synthetic cohorts is almost the same as it would be if nonaffiliation were an age rather than a cohort phenomenon.

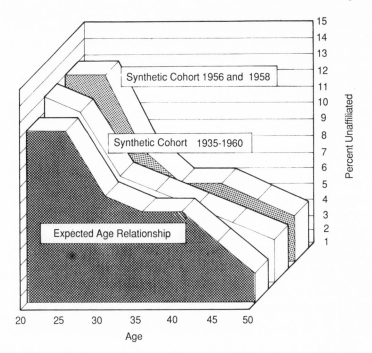

Figure 3.2. No religious affiliation by age for synthetic cohorts.

The "natural" curve of religious nonaffiliation, then, seems to proceed from 12 percent when a group is in its twenties, to 8 percent in its thirties, to 6 percent in its forties, and to 3 percent when it is fifty or older. However, the deviations of a percentage point or two at the youngest age and oldest age levels suggest some net increase in nonaffiliation in younger cohorts, net of age. The standardized beta correlation with cohort, as noted earlier, is .03. The relationship is marginally significant: the null hypothesis (no cohort relationship) can be rejected at the .05 level of significance.

The increase in nonaffiliation is a phenomenon of the 1960s and 1970s. By 1980 it had stopped. It therefore appears to be a "one-shot" change phenomenon instead of a secularization phenomenon (a possibility considered by Glenn, 1987).

Another phenomenon involving an increase during the 1960s

and a leveling-off in the 1980s was the delay in age at marriage and the proportion of the population remaining unmarried. Are the two related? Is the increase in nonaffiliation a demographic and social integration effect? In fact, that appears to be the case. When age at marriage and proportion ever married are introduced into the regression equation, cohort becomes an insignificant factor and the null hypothesis (no relationship between cohort and affiliation) can safely be rejected.

The return to religious affiliation with age (about half of those who were once nonaffiliated seem to return to the affiliation in which they were raised), then, is related to the fact of marriage and to age at marriage. Since we could hardly argue for the opposite explanation—that absence of religious affiliation causes the delay in marriage—we must conclude either that a return to affiliation is the result of marriage (especially when it occurs at a relatively early age) or that marriage and religious affiliation are part of a larger social integration syndrome which varied during the two decades before 1980.

If age at marriage and the proportion of the population never married decline again in subsequent cohorts, we could predict that the marginally significant proportion without religious affiliation would also decline. In each curve there is an increase in those with no affiliation until the age of twenty-five and then a decline until the age of fifty. The earlier people marry, the less likely they are to have no religious affiliation. Those who have not married have the highest level of nonaffiliation.

The increase among younger cohorts in the proportion of people having no religious affiliation—an increase which has leveled off in the last ten years—is not, then, a secularization phenomenon but a demographic one. Marriage and religious affiliation are both "social commitment" variables. A change in culture among the baby boom generation has led to an increase in the number of people who either do not make these commitments at all or make them later in life. In the latter case the effect of the family formation commitment is somewhat less on the religious affiliation commitment.

Who are unaffiliates? Forty-two percent were raised without any affiliation; 5 percent were raised Protestants (less than the 7 percent of "none's" in the population), while 7 percent were raised Catholics, and 9 and 11 percent were raised Jewish and "other" respectively. Thus the "nones" are disproportionately Jewish, "other," and "none" in origin. Yet although there is an "inheritance" correlation—those raised with no religion are more likely than anyone else not to have an affiliation in adult life—more than half of those who were raised with no religious affiliation have found one for themselves.

Not all the unaffiliated are unreligious. Forty-eight percent believe in life after death, 7 percent attend church every month, two-fifths believe in some form of literal interpretation of the Bible, a quarter attend at least once a year, and almost two-fifths go to church at least occasionally.

Half of them describe themselves as politically "liberal" (in contrast to a quarter of the general population). They are also more likely to be politically disaffiliated (in keeping with their disproportionate youthfulness): 55 percent describe themselves as independents, 23 percent as "pure" independents, leaning to neither party (as opposed to 32 percent and 23 percent respectively for the general population).

The increase in "nones," then, is a phenomenon caused by the younger age of the American population, a function of age composition and not a "real" change. The increase in nonmainline Protestants, however, is a real change (as Figure 3.3 demonstrates) and a relatively rapid one. ("Nonmainline" includes Baptist, "other" Protestants, and nondenominational Protestants. I use the term *nonmainline* instead of *fundamentalist* because 43 percent of the group does not accept the strict literal interpretation of the Bible and hence cannot be described as fundamentalist). During the course of the GSS the mainline denominations have decreased from 43 to 40 percent, and the nonmainline groups have increased from 57 to 60 percent.

Unlike the case of those with no religious affiliation, the decline of the mainline groups does correlate significantly with cohort.

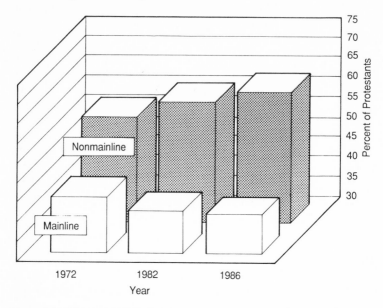

Figure 3.3. Mainline and nonmainline Protestants, 1972–1986 (GSS, 1972, 1982, 1986).

As Figure 3.4 shows, the mainline denominations constitute 45 percent of American Protestants born during the 1920s, but only 28 percent of those born during the 1960s. The Methodists have been especially hard hit by the decline: in the 1920s cohort they were 22 percent of American Protestants; in the 1960s cohort they are 11 percent.

Nor is the decline of mainline Protestantism a function of youthfulness. Within each cohort there is no significant correlation between mainline affiliation and age. Protestants of the mainline denominations do not experiment with other denominations during their younger years and then return to their original denomination as they grow older.

Another way to establish the exodus from the mainline denominations is to compare the religion in which a respondent was raised with the respondent's present religion. Forty-three

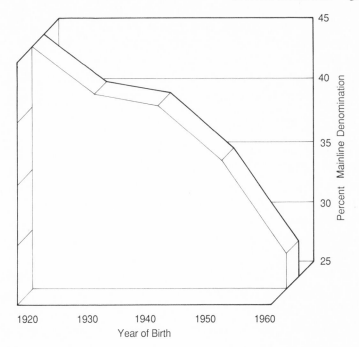

Figure 3.4. Membership in mainline denominations, 1920–1960 (GSS, 1972–
    1987).

percent of American Protestants were raised in the mainline, but
approximately one of every five has moved to the nonmainline
bodies. Fifty-seven percent of Protestant respondents were raised
in nonmainline churches, and one of seven of these has converted
to the mainline. In the exchange (Roof's two flows from liberal
to conservative and conservative to liberal) the mainline loses 3
percentage points and falls to 40 percent of the American Protestant population. A quarter of those raised Methodist and a fifth
of those raised Presbyterian, have moved out of the mainline.
(The Lutherans have lost 11 percent of their members and the
Episcopalians 14 percent.)

About a third of the movement across the mainline-nonmain-
line boundaries can be accounted for by marriage to a spouse

raised on the other side. The rest of the movement away from the mainline seems to be the result of other factors. Over a decade ago Dean M. Kelly (1977) argued that the "other" denominations flourish while the "liberal" denominations decline because the former have greater religious appeal since they have not turned away from "supernatural" religion in favor of social causes. The very political and religious conservatism of the fundamentalist and evangelical denominations makes them appealing to those who still want "religion" from their religion.

The available data provide some support for such an explanation (Table 3.4). The first column represents those who were born in the mainline and have remained there, the second column those who have converted to the mainline from the nonmainline; the third are those who have left the mainline, and the fourth those who were always in the nonmainline. Clearly, respondents in the third column, those who have deserted the mainline, are the most religiously enthusiastic, more likely to attend church, to pray, to picture themselves as strongly religious and as close to God,

Table 3.4.   Religious attitudes and behavior by religious conversion, 1972–1987 (%)

	Once and still mainline	Formerly not mainline but currently mainline	Formerly mainline, now nonmainline	Once and still nonmainline
Attend church 2–3 times/ month	39	50	59	49
Pray several times/day	24	28	47	31
Interpret Bible literally	32	36	53	57
Close to God	28	31	46	37
Strongly religious	36	36	52	48
Support prayer in schools	62	69	71	67
Oppose abortion for poor	41	44	55	59
Member of church-related organization	40	50	52	44

Sources: Pooled data, GSS, 1972–1987.

to support prayer in public schools, and to belong to church-related voluntary organizations than even their nonmainline hosts (in the fourth column). They are somewhat less likely to oppose abortion for the poor and to believe in strict literal interpretation of the Bible.

At the same time those who have moved from the nonmainline denominations into the mainline ones have in most respects assimilated themselves to the religious styles of their "hosts"—although they continue to go to church as regularly as those they have left behind and to support prayer in public schools.

Have the two categories of changers (columns 2 and 3) assimilated to the denomination they have joined, or did they join the new denomination because they found it more appropriate to their own religious style? Obviously such a question cannot be answered with any certainty. We must be content with saying that the move away from the mainline does not indicate any decline in the importance of religion in America, because it represents net gain for those denominations which are apparently more sympathetic to religious enthusiasm. However, only about half of those who have converted away from the mainline accept the literal interpretation of the Bible, a phenomenon which suggests that the enthusiasm of the changers is not quite the same as that of television evangelists.

Thus the data, instead of showing a surge in fundamentalism, suggest a "musical chairs" model: denominational affiliation changes, with the mainline losing some chairs; the more devout leave the mainline for nonmainline denominations, and there is a lesser shift of the less devout into the mainline. The distribution of the Protestant population changes, but the practices and convictions of the population remain the same.

For the four major mainline denominations, however, the situation is obviously critical: they are losing the (apparently) more devout of the recent cohorts to other denominations. As this happens, the levels of religious practice in the mainline may begin to decline, and the defection of those with stronger religious propensities from future cohorts may diminish their proportion of the American population even more.

This change, however, does not mean that fundamentalist denominations are notably increasing. Tom W. Smith of NORC recoded denominational identification in various NORC studies according to "fine-grain" denomination codes (seven Baptist, five Methodist denominations, and so on) (Smith, 1987) to produce a typology of denominations as "Fundamentalist," "Conservative," "Moderate," and "Liberal." He then (Smith, 1988) searched for change in religious affiliation on this variable since 1967 and found no significant increase in the "Fundamentalist" groups. They are about a third of the American population. Nor was there an increase in "Fundamentalist" affiliation among cohorts—about a third of cohorts from 1910 to the present were "Fundamentalist." The "Moderates" increased from 36 percent to 45 percent, and the "Liberals" declined from 32 percent to 21 percent.

Does this picture of American denominationalism mask a decline in the actual strength of religious affiliation? Certainly AIPO measures of "importance of religion" have been volatile in the past several decades. Responses to the questions "At the present time do you think religion as a whole is increasing its influence on American life or losing its influence?" and "Do you believe that religion can answer all or most of today's problems or that religion is old-fashioned and out of date?" have varied greatly in the last three decades.

On the former item, AIPO (1985) reports that those who think religion is increasing its influence plunged from 69 percent in 1957, to 45 percent in 1962, to 14 percent in 1970, and has since rebounded to its 1962 levels.

Leaving aside the issue of the wording of the question (no opportunity for a response that would say "holding its own"), we must still be careful in interpreting this pattern. Normally the annual AIPO release of data on this item occasions headlines such as "Religion Losing Influence" or "Religion Gaining Influence (Again)." Indeed, AIPO itself proclaims: "Uptrend in Religion Increasing Influence" (1985, p. 16). In fact, however, the data reveal nothing about the actual influence of religion (a very intricate matter) but only about the public's *perception* of that increase (or decrease) of influence. The perception is of course itself a reality which deserves to be taken seriously, but it must not be confused with actual influence of religion. (We know the distribution of the perception, but not the extent of the perceived decline. Thus, even if many people perceived only a slight decline, the results would still record a large swing in the perception.)

With the exception of the inexplicable drop from 1957 to 1962, the increase of those saying that religion is "losing its influence" was a phenomenon of the 1960s. The proportion who saw the influence of religion increasing doubled between 1970 and 1974. Hence the item may be an estimate of American society at a given time rather than an estimate of the perceived worth of religion—at least if we can find no evidence of a decrease in personal religious commitment.

Although there is also some volatility between 1974 and 1985 in the proportion who say that religion can answer most of today's problems, that volatility may be as much a judgment on the complexity of the world as it is on religion. Moreover, again there is no middle ground in the AIPO item. Could not a respondent think, on the one hand, that religion is not out of date but on the other that there are many problems in the world for which religion does not have a solution?

Both items do indicate a decline since 1957, but most of the permanent decline occurred between 1957 and 1962. Nonetheless, in an area where stability rather than decline seems to be the rule, a decline in itself is a matter of interest. Moreover, the "influence" item is the only one available that indicates a "cycle" of religious influence. However, because of the "softness" of the items—in both wording and meaning—their results must be compared with those of somewhat firmer measures such as devotional practices. Was there, for example, a decline in church attendance in the late 1950s to parallel and give substance to the declines of positive responses to AIPO "influence"? (In fact Chapter 4 will show that whatever decline there was in church attendance in the last half century occurred after the 1957–1962 period.)

As to the volatility of the "religious influence" item, we must ask whether this changing judgment about religion represents a loss of personal religious commitment or a judgment about the problems of the society. Every year since 1974 GSS, after learning the respondent's denominational affiliation, has asked: "Would you call yourself a strong (religious preference)?" In the fourteen years the question has been asked, the responses have averaged 42 percent saying "strong," 10 percent saying "not strong at all," and the rest saying "somewhat strong." The variations have been only a percentage point up or down. Hence in the era when AIPO has reported great volatility in the perception of religious influence (from 1974 to 1985 a rise from 31 percent to 48 percent in those saying the influence of religion was "increasing"), there has been no change in self-reported intensity of personal religious affiliation. The point is not that the AIPO measure is invalid but that, whatever it measures, it does not measure strength of personal affiliation with one's religious denomination.

Finally, church membership has not changed greatly in the last fifty years. In 1937 AIPO data, 73 percent of Americans "happened to be a member of a church or a synagogue"; in 1947 the figure rose to its high of 76 percent; it fell to its low of 67 percent in 1982 and has risen a couple of percentage points since then (AIPO, 1985). These changes are almost certainly a function of the low rates of membership among the young—58 percent of those under thirty in the 1984 AIPO data reported church membership. Whether lower levels of religious behavior represent a life-cycle or cohort phenomenon will be examined in the next chapter with church attendance as the dependent variable.

America is still a denominational society. The best "fit" for the data is a model which indicates stability of affiliation with the identity Protestant, Catholic, or Jew. In short, denominationalism has not changed much, although patterns of denomi-national affiliation have altered dramatically—despite the fact that levels of conviction and practice are virtually the same as they were forty years ago.

Chapter 4

Church Attendance

In the sociology of religion in Western societies, church attendance has been the classic measure of religious participation. Although it may not indicate the religious symbols by which a person orders and shapes life experiences, attending church or synagogue services on the sabbath is a public affirmation of religious commitment. In Europe church attendance rates have been low for years and are apparently still declining (among the young) in countries such as West Germany and The Netherlands. A decline in regular church attendance in the United States would be taken as a sign of secularization. The Gallup organization has been asking since 1939: "Did you yourself happen to attend church or synagogue in the last seven days?" In 1939, 41 percent replied yes; in 1985 the percentage was 40 (Table 4.1). Consistent patterns of church attendance do not refute a thesis of secularization, but neither do they provide any support for it.

The AIPO data in Table 4.1 also show a decline of 9 percentage points from a high in the late 1950s to 40 percent in 1972, remaining level thereafter. But to analyze this decline it would first of all be necessary to learn who was not going to church. Was it the young, who were a disproportionately large age cohort at that time? Was it Catholics, who were going through the crises of the post–Vatican Council era? Moreover, even the 1972 low is 3 percentage points higher than the previous low of 1940.

NORC has been asking church attendance questions at irregular intervals since 1945, starting six years after AIPO. Since

Table 4.1. Regular church attendance, 1939–1984 (%)

Year	Attended within past 7 days	Year	Attended within past 7 days
1939	41	1972	40
1940	37	1977	41
1950	39	1978	41
1954	46	1979	40
1955	49	1980	40
1957	47	1981	41
1958	49	1982	41
1962	46	1983	40
1967	43	1984	40
1969	42		

Source: AIPO, 1985, p. 42.

1972 it has been inquiring about church attendance every year the GSS has been administered. The NORC question asks how often a respondent attends church, with nine possible response categories: "never," "less than once a year," "about once a year," "several times a year," "about once a month," "2-3 times a month," "nearly every week," "every week," and "several times a week." These categories permit more detailed examination of attendance patterns than does the simple yes/no AIPO question; and when linked with the wide variety of items available in the GSS, the NORC question offers the possibility of an explanation for whatever changes in church attendance that have been occurring.

The AIPO percentage who attended church in the "last seven days" will always be higher than the NORC percentage who attend "every week." Because some people do go to church but not weekly, they will have been inside a church or a synagogue in the last seven days, but not necessarily in the next seven days or in every week for the rest of the year.

The two data sets display a similar long-term pattern for American Protestants and Catholics (Figures 4.1 and 4.2)—a relatively straight line for Protestants, and a sharp dip for Catholics in the late 1960s and early 1970s. Michael Hout and I analyzed the AIPO and NORC data to learn why attendance declined in the late 1960s and then seemed to stop ten years ago (Hout and Greeley, 1987). The model that best fitted the data was one which showed a denomination, age, and year effect for Catholics and an age effect for Protestants. Cohort did not have an effect on the church attendance of either group. Table 4.2 shows a "fitted" model: the "observed" percentage is the actual distribution of respondents; the "expected" percentage is what the numbers would be like if the model fitted reality exactly. The

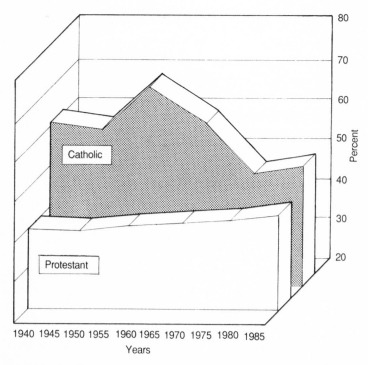

Figure 4.1. Regular church attendance, 1940–1985 (Gallup polls).

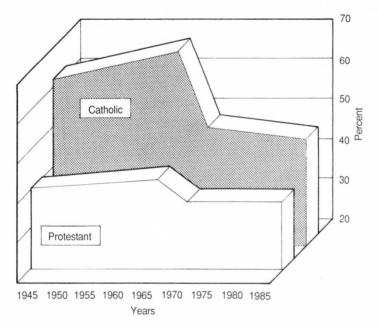

Figure 4.2. Church attendance "nearly every week," 1945–1985 (NORC, 1945–1985).

chances of reality's differing from the model fitted in Table 4.2 are less than .01.

All this means that: (1) whatever changes there are in Protestant churchgoing can be explained merely by the different sizes of the younger age groups at different survey times. Otherwise, Protestant church attendance rates have not changed since 1939. (2) The decline in churchgoing recorded by AIPO was entirely a Catholic phenomenon. In addition to that decline, which could be "naturally" explained by the presence of a large young age group, there was a "year" effect for Catholics, a real decline in church attendance rates. (3) This real decline was not a cohort phenomenon, it was not a change which affected some Catholic age groups more than others. Rather, it was evenly distributed through all age groups. (4) Relative to similar age-related church-

Table 4.2. Observed and expected church attendance, 1940–1980 (%)

Age	Year	Observed		Expected	
		Catholic	Protestant	Catholic	Protestant
20–29	1940	71	34	63	33
	1950	48	28	49	32
	1960	63	29	61	32
	1970	45	35	51	32
	1980	35	33	37	32
30–39	1940	64	35	75	38
	1950	61	32	62	38
	1960	74	40	73	38
	1970	68	38	64	38
	1980	52	42	51	38
40–49	1950	73	40	67	41
	1960	76	44	77	41
	1970	67	41	69	41
	1980	53	41	51	38

Source: Hout and Greeley, 1987, table 1, based on AIPO data.

Note: This model assumes no Protestant change and no cohort effect for either group. Variation is explained by a life-cycle effect and a Catholic year effect.

going among their elders, the younger cohorts (young people born between 1945 and 1960) were not less devout than their predecessors, not the first wave of a "secularist" future.

In sum, the decline in churchgoing in the late 1960s and early 1970s affected only Catholics and was evenly distributed among all age groups.

An analysis of the NORC data confirmed our impression from the AIPO data that there was no discernible cohort effect—no specially irreligious younger generation of Catholics, given the general sharp decline in Catholic churchgoing between 1969 and 1975.

The "religious change" of the late 1960s was a Catholic change, and it is over. The two lines representing Catholic and Protestant attendance continue to march across the page, separated by 10 percentage points now instead of 25, but still persistent.

To test the possible presence of cohort effects—a less religious younger generation—in the decline in Catholic churchgoing between 1969 and 1975, Hout and I prepared a projection of the churchgoing rates of Catholic cohorts old enough to be interviewed in the GSS (up to and including those born in 1964). Comparison of the data with the actual rates of preceding cohorts showed that postconciliar Catholics will not be any less devout— given the populationwide effect of the postconciliar decline. The young people born in the 1960s will not be as devout at the turn of the millennium as were their predecessors in the late 1950s or the early 1960s, before the big decline. But they will be as devout as men and women of that age after the decline. And very few of them will be in the "never" category of church attendance.

Two questions remain to be answered: Why did the Catholic church attendance decline—sharp, dramatic, and sudden—begin? And why did it end?

The most obvious response would be that the decline was the result of the changes effected by the Second Vatican Council and that it ended because the effects of the council finally were spent. However, such a response is nothing more than a guess until data are produced to substantiate it.

In fact, the story is much more complex and reveals a fascinating dimension of American religion. Catholic church attendance declined because of birth control, and the decline ended because of the "loyalty" of the Catholics who continued to attend church regularly despite rejection of the official teaching on birth control. The story behind the sharp downward movement in Figures 4.1 and 4.2 fits none of the five models described in Chapter 1. It is rather a story of American Catholics going through their own quiet revolution of deciding to remain Catholic on their own terms, a phenomenon which reveals a great deal about American religion but which does not fit any of the currently popular models of the sociology of religion.

First of all, the erosion of Catholic church attendance did not begin immediately after the end of Vatican II, but in 1969, four years after the council adjourned and the year after Pope Paul

VI's famous encyclical letter on birth control *(Humanae Vitae)*, which reaffirmed, in the face of widespread Catholic hopes for a change, the traditional teaching against all forms of "artificial" contraception. The timing of the decline therefore suggests that perhaps the cause was not the council (save perhaps in that the council raised hopes for a change in birth control doctrine), but the encyclical.

In 1976 William McCready, Kathleen McCourt, and I were able to demonstrate that all of the 16-percentage-point decline could be accounted for by the influx of a younger age cohort (of very substantial size) and a parallel decline in acceptance of papal infallibility and of birth control teaching (Greeley, McCready, and McCourt, 1976). There were three possible explanations for this mathematically demonstrated relationship: the authority and birth-control ethic decline caused the church attendance decline; the church attendance decline caused the erosion of support for authoritative teaching; both were caused by some prior variable. The second possibility is inherently improbable: you don't take the birth control pill because and merely because you've stopped going to church. Whether the first or third explanation is true does not matter for the purposes of this discussion, because even if there were a prior variable at work it would still link the birth control encyclical to church attendance erosion.

Hout and I (1987) reanalyzed the data from the two Catholic studies of 1963 and 1974 (Greeley, McCready, and McCourt, 1976) using the new analytic models developed during the past ten years. Table 4.3 shows the results. The final column shows what attendance rates would have been in 1974 given the 1963 relationship between churchgoing and birth control and attitudes toward authority and the decline in these latter two items between 1963 and 1974. The resemblance between the observed and hypothetical attendance for 1974 indicates that, if one had known in 1963 that Catholics would so drastically change their minds about birth control and papal authority, one could have predicted Catholic churchgoing rates in 1974 with astonishing accuracy.

Table 4.3. Observed and hypothetical Catholic church attendance, 1963 and 1974 (%)

Attendance	Observed 1963	Observed 1974	Hypothetical 1974
Never	6	13	12
Yearly	12	20	19
Monthly	12	17	16
Weekly	71	51	53

Source: Hout and Greeley, 1987.

Table 4.4. Weekly Catholic church attendance by confidence in clergy and attitudes toward premarital sex, 1974–1983 (%)

Year	High confidence in clergy[a]		Low confidence in clergy	
	Approve of premarital sex	Disapprove of premarital sex[b]	Approve of premarital sex	Disapprove of premarital sex[b]
1974	23	50	34	71
1975	24	48	45	68
1977	26	57	37	66
1978	23	53	50	72
1982	26	48	30	66
1983	27	47	37	76

Source: Hout and Greeley, 1987, based on GSS data.

a. Respondents who report "a great deal of confidence in church leaders" are rated "high."

b. Respondents who disapprove of premarital sex are those who say it is "always wrong" or "almost always wrong."

Hout and I then turned to the GSS, which provided different measures for attitudes toward sexuality and toward teaching authority—judgments about premarital sex and about confidence in religious leadership. (We first established that the proportion of those who were born Catholic and continue to describe themselves as Catholic had not changed from 1972 to 1985—85 percent in both years.) As Table 4.4 shows, there is a powerful relationship between these attitudes and churchgoing for Catholics (although, as Hout noted, even those who reject the birth-control ethic and have little confidence in church leaders do not completely abandon church attendance—only 10 percent in this "double negative" category "never" go to church). Moreover, we could not reject the model which said that the effects from 1972 to 1975 in Catholic churchgoing could be accounted for by attitudes on authority and sexuality.

But only half the problem was resolved. Catholic acceptance of premarital sex continued to increase after 1975, but the decline in churchgoing stopped. What happened?

One afternoon Hout and I noticed that the graphs depicting Catholic churchgoing rates (Figures 4.1 and 4.2) looked remarkably similar to a graph (Figure 7.1) depicting Catholic affiliation with the Democratic party—there was a sharp decline in the late 1960s which tapered off in the mid-1970s. Could they be related phenomena? Sure enough, strength of affiliation with either party does indeed correlate with strength of churchgoing propensity (Table 4.5). Among "strong" political identifiers the decline in churchgoing was 12 percentage points from 1972 to 1975 and none thereafter. Among "weak" Democrats or Republicans there was a 17-percentage-point drop from 1972 to 1984; among independents who "leaned" one way or another the decline was 19 percentage points from 1972 to 1975, with some rebound thereafter. Among pure independents, 63 percent attended church weekly or nearly weekly in 1972, but only 29 percent in 1984—a decline of 34 percent. The weaker the party affiliation, the greater the decline in churchgoing for Catholics during the trying times after the Second Vatican Council and the encyclical.

Sociologists speak of "latent" structures, variables which we postulate as underlying a relationship between two variables which are clearly linked but which are not likely to have a causal effect on each other. Hout and I postulated such a latent structure which we called "loyalty," meaning a propensity to stick to an institution (or a community) in the face of trouble—in this case,

Table 4.5. Weekly Catholic church attendance by strength of political affiliation, 1972–1984 (%)

Year	Independent	Leaning	Weak	Strong
1972	63	57	58	68
1973	44	57	47	47
1974	49	45	49	60
1975	33	38	50	56
1976	40	37	44	51
1977	44	46	49	58
1978	35	56	42	59
1980	38	43	48	64
1982	24	31	44	53
1983	37	46	44	50
1984	29	49	41	57

Source: Hout and Greeley, 1987, table 12, based on GSS data.

the influence of George McGovern in the Democratic party and Pope Paul VI's birth control encyclical.

It is one thing to postulate such an underlying dimension and another thing to establish by rigorous methods the probability of its existence. Using a model developed by the Swiss statistician Georg Rasch (1960) and refined by Otis Dudley Duncan (1985), we fitted our loyalty assumption to extremely precise and rigorous testing. The model specified not only the distribution of data but also the distribution of data on religious and political affiliation if there was the kind of "latent" structure in the direction we expected between the latent structure and both political affiliation and religious devotion. Unless the fit between the data and the model was extremely tight, the model would have to be rejected. We were, however, not able to reject it. Therefore, such a latent loyalty structure best explains the relationship between the two known variables.

Thus there does seem to be a variable which links political and religious loyalty and which behaves mathematically as such a variable ought to behave. Interestingly, it relates more strongly to religion than to party affiliation and distinguishes most sharply between those who "never" go to church or are "pure" independents leaning in the direction of neither party and the rest of the population. The real break from loyalty comes when a person gives up churchgoing completely or chooses to affiliate with neither political party, not even to the extent of "leaning" toward one or the other.

The "loyalty" variable, in other words, put a brake on the decline of Catholic churchgoing in the mid-1970s. About a third of the regular Catholic churchgoers who rejected the birth control teaching (only 15 percent of Catholics accept it), it would seem, were so offended by the birth control decision that they stopped going to church regularly (though usually not completely). But the other two-thirds, when apparently faced with a choice between a drift to the margins of the church and acceptance of the birth control encyclical, chose neither. They would remain regular churchgoers, but on their own terms, rejecting the official teaching but still showing up at church every week or nearly every week. They did so for the same reason that Catholics remained loyal to their political party (mostly but not all Democrats) at least until 1980, despite candidates for the presidency for whom they had no taste.

It would appear that the religious mechanism by which they justified their loyalty was an appeal to a God who "understood" instead of to church leaders who did not. Moreover, those Catholics who were most likely to think of themselves as "close" to God were best able to cope with juggling regular church attendance and rejection of the birth control teaching.

More research on the loyalty variable is needed, but it suffices for our purposes here to say that a kind of "ethnic" loyalty has held large numbers of Catholics to regular church attendance despite the traumas of the past twenty years and has apparently reestablished a stable pattern of church attendance for them— perhaps because, as Herberg observed long ago, in America you have to be something. Being Catholic is part of being American, it is a way of fitting into American society, it is one of the definitions and social locations you apply to yourself. It is your parish church and your friends and your family. Give it up? Don't be silly.

"Did you hear about Councilman Murphy?" says one Irish woman to another in the back of the church on Sunday (Glazer and Moynihan, 1963, p. 19):

"What's he done now?"

"He's become a Republican."

"Ah sure, that can't be true. I saw him right here at Mass last Sunday!"

The model in that story doesn't quite fit our data. Political loyalty in either direction (Democratic or Republican) correlates with religious loyalty. Or rather, both correlate with an underlying "loyalty" dimension in our pluralistic society in which it seems to many of us that you must belong to a number of relatively

able 4.6. Church attendance and life cycle, 1963 and 1985 (%)

	Catholic (N = 3116)				Protestant (N = 7939)	
	1963		1985		1985	
ge	Weekly	Never[a]	Weekly	Never[a]	Weekly	Never[a]
3–19	67	17	30	13	29	18
⊃–24	59	7	25	15	28	17
5–29	68	8	30	15	28	17
⊃–34	71	6	36	14	33	19
5–39	71	6	49	13	36	19
⊃–44	71	5	51	11	34	18
5–49	74	5	48	13	38	17
⊃–54	71	4	57	12	43	19
5–59	82	4	60	11	38	18
⊃–64			64	9	40	18
5–70			61	12	41	18

Sources: 1963: NORC (which did not include respondents over sixty); 1985: pooled data of GSS, 1975–⊃85.

a. "Never" includes those who attend "less than once a year."

primary groups if you are going to be anyone. But the story illustrates the point, and both indicate directions for further research and give a hint of an explanation for the other phenomena reported here: religion persists in America, relatively unchanged for the past half-century, in part because the social structures of American society positively if unintentionally reinforce religion, the exact opposite of what seems to be the case in many European countries.

Because there is no cohort effect on American church attendance, and because Catholic churchgoing has stabilized since the 1970s, it is possible to plot life-cycle church attendance rates (Table 4.6).

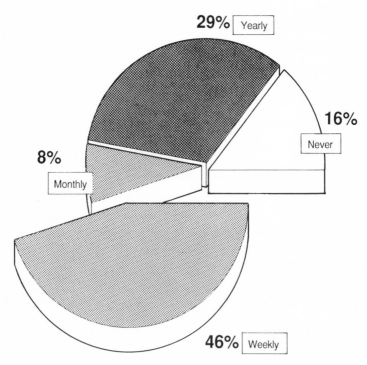

Figure 4.3. Protestant church attendance for those between 40 and 45, 1972–1986 (GSS, 1972, 1986).

There is little difference between Protestant and Catholic churchgoing when young men and women are in their twenties—less than a third attend church every week. However, a higher level of Catholic attendance begins to appear during the thirties. After forty the lead is well over 10 percentage points in each age group. By the time men and women are in their early forties, 51 percent of Catholics and 34 percent of Protestants are going to church every week or almost every week. If we add those who attend at least once a month, half the Protestants and two-thirds of the Catholics (52 and 67 percent, respectively) are in church at least one Sunday a month (Figures 4.3, 4.4). However, even in the early twenties 48 percent of Protestants and 47 percent of

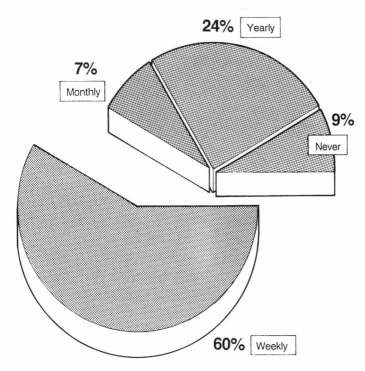

Figure 4.4. Catholic church attendance for those between 40 and 45, 1972–1986 (GSS, 1972, 1986).

Catholics attend church at least that often. The increase, more striking among Catholics, in regular church attendance does not represent the return of the totally alienated but rather more regular attendance by the already irregularly attending. The rates of those attending "never" (which includes "less than once a year") do not change notably with age for either group.

The Catholic life-cycle relationship with church attendance is much tighter today than it was in 1963. However, the difference disappears when one considers the proportion who go to church at least once a month—half of those under twenty-five and almost two-thirds of those in their early forties. The result of *Humanae Vitae* in the United States was not so much to drive Catholics away from church attendance as to make that attendance somewhat more irregular than it had been.

With the exception of the dramatic Catholic change between 1968 and 1975 (an episodic event), patterns of American church attendance are remarkably stable—straight lines with only one deviation, and that ended by 1975.

Secularization that is not.

Chapter 5

Devotions, Defections, Activities, and Attitudes

This chapter examines a miscellany of other religious measures to see if they are as stable as church attendance rates—prayer, religious experience, membership in church-related organizations, intermarriage and defection rates, and attitudes toward members of other religious groups. For most of these measures the time series is not as long as it is for church attendance. However, we can at least investigate short- and medium-range trends.

In 1972, when NORC first asked its question about prayer—"How often do you pray?"—in a national study of American religion (McCready and Greeley, 1975), 54 percent of respondents said they prayed every day, and half of that group said they prayed more than once a day. The question was inserted in GSS beginning in 1983 on the theory that prayer might be a better measure of personal religious devotion and commitment than church attendance. In 1983, 57 percent of GSS respondents reported daily prayer, and 59 percent in 1985. During this period, the percentage reporting prayer more than once a day rose from 24 to 27 percent. On the other hand, some 20 percent of respondents in the early 1970s and mid-1980s said they prayed less than once a week, while 2 percent reported that they never prayed.

In the mid-1980s some three-fourths of Americans surveyed prayed at least once a week, almost three-fifths prayed every day, and more than a quarter prayed several times a day. Sixteen percent of those with no religious affiliation prayed every day, and a third of them prayed at least once a week. If some 95 percent of Americans believe in God, but only 2 percent never pray, then there is a small fraction of the population which prays to a God in whose existence they have considerable doubt—a useful form of insurance, perhaps.

AIPO's somewhat less precise question—"Do you ever pray to God?"—elicited a 90 percent positive response in 1948 and an 87 percent positive response in 1985; thus, the AIPO data indicate a somewhat higher proportion of nonprayers than does GSS—13 percent in 1985 for AIPO and 2 percent for GSS. AIPO also reports (1985) that 31 percent pray twice a day or more, a few percentage points higher than the 28 percent reported in the same year by GSS. AIPO adds that this figure represents a decline from higher rates of more frequent prayer in 1952 and 1965, when some two-fifths of Americans prayed twice a day or more. NORC data on prayer do not go back to the time before 1970, and the different wording of the questions makes strict comparison dubious, but both AIPO and NORC indicate an increase in the rate of more than daily prayer from the early 1970s to the mid-1980s, from 27 to 31 percent for AIPO (1978 to 1985) and from 25 percent to 29 percent for NORC/GSS (1972–1985).

The only issue that might persist in the face of the different wording of questions is whether the presently observed high rates of prayer represent a rebound from somewhat lower rates two decades ago or continuity with previous rates which were already quite high and some increase over those rates. Neither survey organization can find evidence of a decline in American prayer.

Americans, then, are more likely to pray daily than they are to go to church weekly, as likely to pray as to believe in God (perhaps even more likely to pray than to believe in God), and considerably more likely to pray more than once a day than to have sexual intercourse every day.

The options, then, are either stability of prayer rates or an increase in them. There is once more no evidence of secularization.

In its national study of American religion in 1972, NORC initiated a project to study the prevalence and incidence of mystical and psychic experiences in American society. The question about mystical experiences was: "Have you ever felt as though you were very close to a powerful spiritual force that seemed to lift you out of yourself?" Approximately a third of Americans reported such experiences in 1972 (almost exactly the same proportion as reported in the extensive studies done by Sir Alastair Hardy, David Hay, and their colleagues in extensive research in Great Britain; Hay and Morisy, 1978). Five percent reported that such experiences had occurred "often." When these mystical and parapsychological questions were repeated in the 1984 GSS, the proportion reporting ecstatic experiences had risen to 40 percent, with 7 percent of respondents saying that such experiences had occurred often in their lives. Like prayer, intense religious experiences (or the reporting of them) have increased since the early 1970s.

Whether such experiences are "religious" indicators or not may be problematic, but there are also increases on the parapsychological items. In 1972 some 60 percent of respondents reported that they had thought they "were somewhere you had been before but knew that it was impossible." In 1984 the proportion had increased to 67 percent. A similar increase, from 60 percent to 67 percent, was recorded in response to the question; "Have you ever felt as though you were in touch with someone when they were far away from you?" In the early 1970s 25 percent said they had "seen events that happened at a great distance as they were happening." In the mid-1980s this rate had risen to 30 percent. Finally, in 1972 25 percent reported that they had "felt as though you were really in touch with someone who had died." This proportion rose 17 percentage points to 42 percent in 1984.

Obviously such responses raise a number of fascinating questions, most of which, however interesting, are unrelated to our investigation. The issue for those involved in this research at NORC is not whether such "psychic" experiences are "real" but rather the rates at which incidents are reported and the correlates, the antecedents, and the consequences of such experiences. For our purposes here, one need merely say that there is no evidence in the available data for a decline in awareness of or sensitivity to what might be broadly called the "supernatural" during the last decade and a half. On the contrary, the increase in prayer and in mystical and psychic experiences suggests that, if anything, such sensitivity has increased, or at least a willingness, not to say eagerness, to report it.

Membership in church-related voluntary organizations is as stable as the other religious indicators analyzed so far. In 1960 an AIPO survey reported that 35 percent of Americans belonged to a church-related group. NORC has included a similar item in the GSS since 1974. In the early 1970s the proportion affiliated with a church-related group had risen to 40 percent, but in the late 1970s it had declined again to 37 percent and in the early 1980s to 36 percent, still higher than AIPO had recorded in 1960. Church-related organizations continue to attract more members than any other voluntary organizations in the United States.

The final issue in this chapter is whether the boundaries of religious groups in America have become more permeable either because of the popularity of ecumenism or perhaps because of an increase in religious "indifference"—a perception that one religion is more or less as good (or as bad) as any other. Three indicators can help to shed light on this question of religious boundaries: rates of change of affiliation, rates of mixed marriage, and changes in attitudes toward other religions.

First of all, if we look beyond the data presented in Table 3.3 on percentages of denominational change, we find that defection rates among the major religious groupings, with the exception of the Methodists, have not increased in the years of the GSS (Table 5.1). Nor has the "net loss" (defectors minus converts) changed—Protestants and Catholics have a 2 percent net loss in both 1972 and 1985. Second, the proportion of respondents

Table 5.1. Rates of religious change, 1972–1985

	Protestant		Catholic		Jewish	
	1972	1985	1972	1985	1972	1985
Defection rate[a]	9	9	15	16	15	15
Net loss[b]	2	2	2	2	—	—
Mixed marriage[c]	11	11	23	21	8	17

Sources: NORC/GSS, pooled data for 1972–1975 and 1982–1985.

a. The number who were in a given group at sixteen and are no longer a member of the group, divided by the total who were in the religious group when they were sixteen.

b. Defection rate minus those who were in another group at sixteen and have now joined the group being considered: converts minus defectors.

c. The proportion of those married to a member of another group divided by all the married respondents of one's own group.

Table 5.2. Denominational defection rates, 1972 and 1985 (%)

Denomination	1972	1985
Baptist	26	26
Episcopalian	42	40
Lutheran	29	29
Methodist	36	40
Presbyterian	47	42

Source: GSS, 1972 and 1985.

presently living in religiously mixed marriages has not changed: approximately one-tenth for Protestants and one-fifth for Catholics. (Johnson, 1985, in an intensive and complex study of religious associative marriages reports that even though higher social and economic status has increased the likelihood of exogamy for Catholics in the last fifty years, the actual rates have not changed.)

Third, within the Protestant grouping and among the Protestant denominations there is considerable movement from denomination to denomination (Table 5.2). This movement results in a decline in mainline denominations (especially the Methodists) but little change in the levels of religious behavior.

Denominational good feeling, as far as the available data indicate, has not led to a collapse of religious boundaries during the 1970s and the 1980s. The only time-series measure of interreligious attitudes is the SRC election research "thermometer" question, which asks respondents to rate their feelings toward certain groups on a scale from zero to 100, with the high number expressing positive feelings and the low number less positive feelings. The three major American religious groupings were included in these measures in five election surveys from 1960 to 1976. In 1986 the question was added to the GSS.

There are advantages and disadvantages to the "thermometer" items. On the one hand, because they lack substantive content, their precise meaning is difficult if not impossible to interpret. On the other hand, they probably measure raw and instinctive emotional reactions better than specific content items.

Figures 5.1, 5.2, and 5.3 summarize the results of an analysis of how members of the three major American religious groupings felt about one another from 1964 to 1984. A ranking above 70 on the scale of 0–100 was rated as "warm." Four observations can be made:

1. Catholics have warmer feelings toward Protestants and Jews than the latter groups have toward Catholics.

2. Jews and Protestants have warmer feelings toward each other than they do toward Catholics.

3. Good feelings among the three groups went up during the years 1968–1972 despite the turbulence of those times in American society (and despite the perceived decline in the influence of religion reported by AIPO). This increase might be the result of the ecumenical goodwill generated by the Second Vatican Council. If such was the case, however, there was no particular payoff for Catholics: they continued to be the least liked and the most liking of the three religious groupings.

4. Finally, good mutual feelings declined sharply among all three groups in the years between the 1972 and 1976 elections.

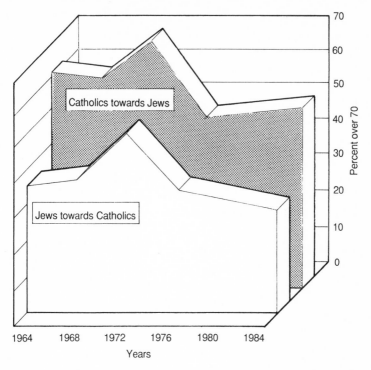

Figure 5.1. Warm feelings between Catholics and Jews, 1964–1984 (SRC, GSS, national election years).

This decline, however, was matched by parallel changes on non-religious SRC "thermometer" measures, so it apparently reflects a societywide phenomenon and not a purely interreligious one. Perhaps it represents a residue of ill will in the society over the last stages of the process of attempting to impeach and then pardoning a president. In 1986 Protestant and Catholic feelings toward each other had converged, and Catholic warm feelings toward Jews had increased, though not to the level of the early 1970s. However, the 1986 data suggest that the high levels of warm feelings reported by all groups in the early 1970s seem untypical.

Nonetheless, the convergence between Protestants and Cath-

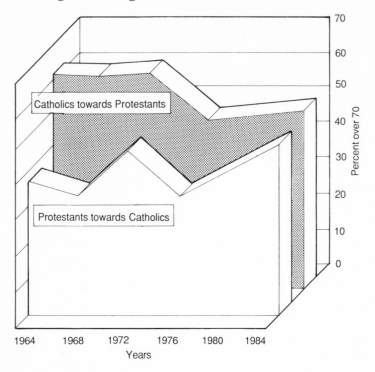

Figure 5.2. Warm feelings between Catholics and Protestants, 1964–1984
(SRC, GSS, national election years).

olics in 1986 does represent a statistically significant change—a
change achieved by a decline in Catholic warm feelings for Protestants and an increase in Protestant warm feelings for Catholics.

These "thermometer" measures without substantive content
do not justify the assertion that, with the exception of the Prot-
estant-Catholic convergence, little has changed in American interreligious attitudes since 1960. They merely prove that we have
no data currently available to establish that there has been change.
Of more serious concern is the hint that Catholics have been
better disposed toward other groups but no more likely to receive
goodwill. Perhaps the convergence between Catholics and Protestants in 1984 represents a more realistic evaluation of the situation by both groups.

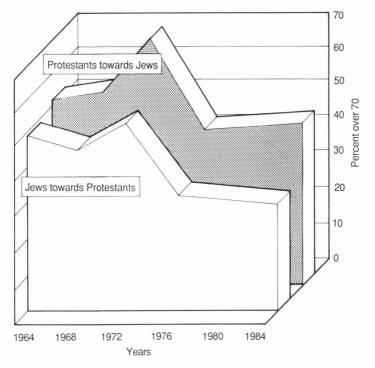

Figure 5.3. Warm feelings between Jews and Protestants, 1964–1984 (SRC, GSS, national election years).

There are no data in this chapter which fit the secularization model. Interreligious attitudes tend to move in irregular patterns for which we have yet no satisfactory explanation. Prayer and the reporting of religious and psychic experiences have actually increased since 1972, although there may have been a decline in prayer twice a day or more before 1972, from which there is now a rebound. Rates of participation in church-related voluntary organizations are the same as they were in 1960 and continue to be much higher than in any other kind of voluntary organizations. The boundaries among religious groupings as measured by religious mixed marriages, conversion and defection rates, and interreligious attitudes do not seem to have changed since 1972.

The analysis in the first five chapters indicates that about two-fifths of the American population are quite religious (they pray and go to church regularly and participate in religious organizations); another two-fifths are somewhat religious (they pray and attend church, but not so regularly; they do not participate in religious associations but do accept major doctrinal tenets); and another one-fifth are rather unreligious (they rarely pray or go to church and do not believe in life after death or the divinity of Jesus but still believe in God). These proportions do not seem to have changed greatly in the years for which we have data.

Chapter 6

Financial Contributions

Sociologists have paid little attention to financial contributions to one's church as a measure of religious devotion. In American society, however, based as it is on a voluntaristic approach to religion, donations to one's parish or congregation are an excellent indicator of the importance of religion in a person's life. There is no legal force to compel a contribution; yet without the contributions of their people, local churches cannot long survive. A decline in the amount of one's annual contribution to one's church would indicate a lessening of the intensity of institutional affiliation. On the other hand, the persistence of the same level of giving over a sustained period would suggest durability and continuity of religious affiliation.

William McManus and I explored the trends in financial contributions among Protestants and Catholics since 1960 (Greeley and McManus, 1987). There are six data sets available to address this issue: two from SRC at the University of Michigan (Morgan et al., 1962 and 1979), two from the 1963 and 1974 NORC studies of the effects of Catholic education, a 1983 AIPO study, and a final study of American philanthropy executed by the Yankelovich organization for the Independent Sector (White, 1986). The contribution findings in the 1960 SRC study and the 1963 NORC study (limited to Catholics) do not differ statistically, nor do the results of the 1974 NORC study and the 1975 SRC study. Thus the measures in the early 1960s and mid-1970s of independent projects confirm one another. Finally, the two 1980s studies validate each other. Thus there are two data sets at each major point on the time continuum: early 1960s, mid-1970s, and mid-1980s.

In the early 1960s American Protestants and Catholics gave about the same amount of money to their churches in annual contributions, $141 from Catholics and $138 from Protestants (the 1960 dollar could buy in goods and services what three and a half dollars purchase today). In the mid-1970s the Protestant contribution had risen to $262 and the Catholic to $179. In the mid-1980s, Catholics were giving on the average $320 and Protestants on the average $580 (in 1984 dollars). Catholic contributions had doubled in the quarter-century but had fallen behind the inflation curve (Figure 6.1), while Protestant contributions had quadrupled and kept pace with the inflation curve.

Thus in 1963 both Protestants and Catholics gave 2.2 percent of their annual income to their respective churches. In 1973 Protestants were still giving 2.2 percent, while Catholic gifts had declined to 1.6 percent of their annual income. In 1983 Protestant contributions continued at the 2.2 percent rate while Catholic contributions had declined to 1.1 percent of their income (Figure 6.2). Both the decline from 1963 to 1973 and from 1973 to 1983 are statistically significant. So too are the differences between Catholics and Protestants at the latter two time points. Once more, then, we encounter the phenomenon of Protestant continuity and Catholic decline. However, unlike the decline in church attendance, the Catholic decline in financial contribution did not stop in the middle 1970s.

This decline is the sharpest among those who attend mass every week—from 2.69 percent of annual income in 1963 to 2.15 percent in 1973 to 1.69 percent in 1983. Many Catholics therefore continued to be ritually devout while sharply curtailing their financial commitments to the institutional church.

The difference between Catholics and Protestants in 1984 contributions are consistent in every age, educational, economic, and family size group—with the differences especially great among

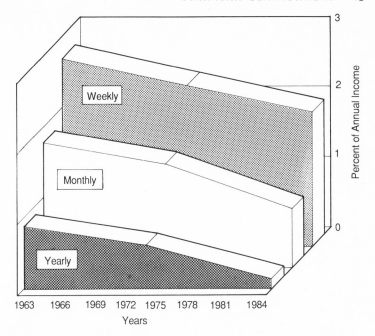

Figure 6.1. Annual contributions of Catholics by church attendance, 1963–1984 (NORC, 1963–1974; White, 1986).

those who are better educated and more affluent, and who have the smallest families. Among those who go to church every week, Protestants who earn less than $20,000 a year give about twice as much as their Catholic counterparts, Protestants who earn $20,000–40,000 a year give almost three times as much, and Protestants who earn more than $40,000 annually give more than four times as much (Figure 6.3). If we assume that Catholics make up approximately a quarter of the population, constituting about 21 million families and unrelated individuals, these findings suggest that the current annual loss to the Catholic church from the decline of lay contributions is close to $6 billion. Over the quarter-century the loss is approximately $65 billion.

The decline is sharpest among the more "liberal" Catholics—

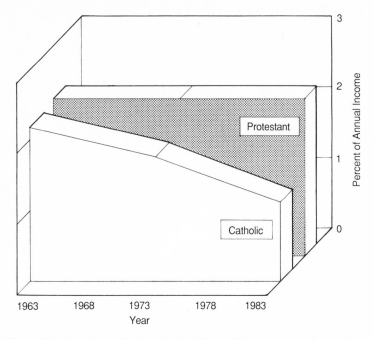

Figure 6.2. Annual contributions by Catholics and Protestants, 1963–1983
(SRC, 1968, 1978; NORC, all years; White, 1986).

those who support an obligation to work for racial justice, those who reject the church's teaching on birth control, and those who support government concern for the poor.

In 1963, Catholics who thought that there was a personal obligation to work for the end of racial segregation gave 2.2 percent of their income to the church, the same amount as those who did not think there was such an obligation. In 1974 the contributions of the former fell to 1.3 percent, of the latter to 1.7 percent.

There was not a comparably worded question in the 1984 research, but Catholics who thought that the government should guarantee food and shelter to the needy gave 1.1 percent of their income to the church, while those who did not think the gov-

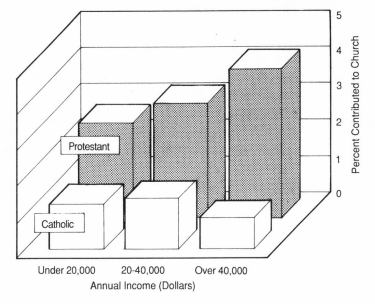

Figure 6.3. Contributions to church by income and denomination (weekly attenders), 1960–1985 (White, 1986).

ernment should be concerned about such matters gave 2 percent. (There was no difference among Protestants which related to attitudes toward government help to the poor.)

In 1963 those who accepted the church's teaching on birth control gave 2.3 percent of their annual earnings to the church, while those who did not gave 2.0 percent (Figure 6.4). Eleven years later the former group was still contributing 2.1 percent, while the latter (which had increased in size from half to seven-eighths of the Catholic population) was giving only 1.5 percent.

One way to visualize the impact of the change in birth control attitudes on contributions is to ask how much Catholics would be giving today if the decline in contributions had been similar in the two birth control attitude groups. Projecting the 1963–1974 line to 1984 (Figure 6.5), we see that the decline would have been to 1.7 percent of income.

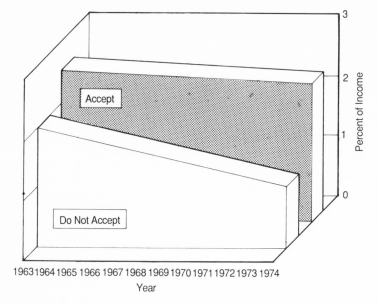

Figure 6.4. Catholic contributions by acceptance of birth control doctrine, 1963–1974 (NORC).

To account for a change with survey analysis techniques three things must occur: (1) The explanatory (independent) variable must be related to the variable to be explained (birth control attitudes and church contributions); (2) both variables must change; and (3) the correlation must persist or grow strong. In this case the correlation not merely persists but increases: those who rejected the birth control teaching in 1974 would have given much less in comparison to those who accepted it than was the case in 1963.

Figure 6.6 shows the results of a mathematical model analysis of the change in Catholic contributions from 1963 to 1974. Fourteen percent of the decline could be attributed to the erosion of attendance at mass, 15 to the influx into the population of a younger and less generous age group, 12 percent to changing attitudes on papal authority, and 38 percent to a decline in

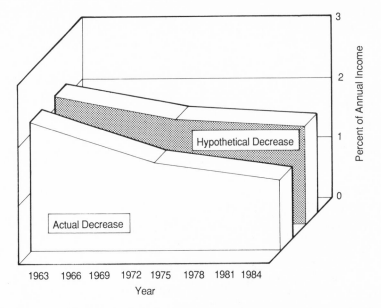

Figure 6.5. Projected Catholic contributions if decline had been the same for those who accepted and rejected birth control doctrine, 1963–1984 (NORC, 1963, 1984).

acceptance of Catholic sexual ethics. A final 21 percent of the change was not accounted for by the model.

Half of the 1963–1974 decline, then, can be accounted for by changing Catholic attitudes on sex and authority. Because there was no question on sexual ethics in the 1984 Yankelovich study, we cannot assert with total confidence that the principal engine driving Catholic contributions downward in the first half of the period was still at work in the second half. As we shall see shortly, respect for the official teaching continues to erode—now more on the subject of premarital sex than on birth control or divorce. Moreover, financial contributions continue to decline at the same rate as they did in the first half of the period. If the two decreases are no longer linked, then another, unknown engine has intervened to power the two declines. Such a phenomenon is not

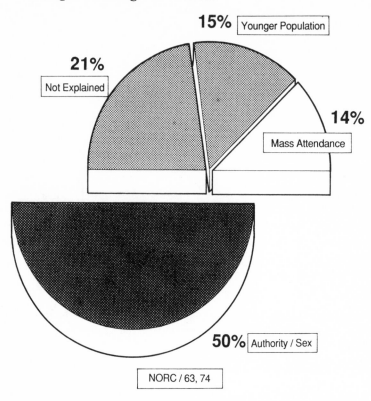

Figure 6.6. Explanation of decline in Catholic contributions, 1963–1974
(NORC, 1963, 1974).

impossible, but it is highly unlikely: it requires a new factor to account for half of the continuing decline in contributions.

Once again whatever change has occurred in American religious behavior is restricted to Catholics. While Protestant contributions remain stable, Catholics appear to be partially alienated from the institutional church. On the one hand, they participate in weekly church attendance and other forms of ritual and community activity, but on the other hand they reject certain church teachings and give only half of what they once did to the support of the ecclesiastical institution.

It remains to be seen when and if this decline will bottom out.

The episodic event model seems to account for the changes in Catholic contributions, the continuity model for Protestant contributions. There is no support for the secularization model in patterns of church contributions.

Chapter 7

Social Status and Political Affiliation

In previous chapters religion has been the dependent variable: we have asked what effect time, age, and cohort have on religion as it is defined by beliefs, attitudes, and practices. This chapter and the next consider religion as an independent or "predictor" variable—the effect religion itself has had on social and political and ethical attitudes and behavior. We will be asking in effect two questions—does religion differentiate among Americans in these attitudes and behaviors, and has that differential effect changed during the years in which time series measures have been available?

This chapter focuses on the relationship between religion and two sets of behaviors—success and politics—and possible changes in the strength of the religious impact on these behaviors. Because there are too few Jewish respondents, even in the GSS, we cannot discuss with any confidence a possible change in their economic and educational success and their political liberalism over time; hence comparisons will be restricted to Catholics and Protestants. Is it true that Catholicism has been and remains an obstacle to success in American life? Are Catholics in fact more conservative than Protestants, and is this conservatism increasing or decreasing? Is the traditional Catholic alliance with the Democratic party weakening as the party becomes more liberal and Catholics continue to be conservative (or perhaps become more conservative)?

Much ink has been spilled on these issues in the last quarter-century. Since Max Weber published his classic *The Protestant Ethic and the Spirit of Capitalism* in 1904, sociologists have tried to find evidence that in the United States as in the Germany Weber studied, Protestants are more likely to be successful than Catholics. The "dogmatism" of Catholic faith, the "authoritarianism" of Catholic discipline, the "rigidity" of Catholic thought, the "otherworldliness" of Catholic piety, the size of Catholic families, and the "repressiveness" of Catholic education have all been cited as explanations for lower Catholic social and economic achievement.

Because educational decisions and occupational choices are usually made in one's late teens or early twenties, we can determine roughly what decisions were being made in given decades of this century by considering the educational and occupational achievements of those who were in their early twenties at that time. In the years 1910–1919, for example, young men and women born in the decade 1890–1899 were deciding whether to go to college and what kind of a career to pursue. By surveying the ratio of white Catholic choice to white Protestant choice over several decades we can ascertain whether the Catholic population, heavily immigrant until 1920, has begun to catch up with nativeborn white Protestants. It may be argued that Catholics would be more likely to "catch up" in college attendance and perhaps also in occupational decisions later in life, through night school and similar efforts. Thus the ratio of Catholic to Protestant college attendance as measured in the 1890–1899 birth cohort may understate the actual differences in the early decades of this century. However, the pertinent question is whether there is evidence of an increasing ratio and not whether all of the increase can be accounted for by young adult decisions.

Table 7.1 presents the ratios for college attendance, professional careers, and white-collar employment. Thus the ratio of .70 for college attendance in 1910–19 means that the proportion of Catholics going to college in the 1920s was seven-tenths of the proportion of Protestants. The figure of 1.43 for 1980–85

Table 7.1.   Ratio of Catholic to white Protestant achievement by cohort, 1910–1985

Years of decision[a]	Attended college	Professional[b]	White collar[c]
1910–19	.70	.65	.93
1920–29	.62	.81	.97
1930–39	.90	.90	1.04
1940–49	.92	.88	1.02
1950–59	.96	1.07	1.02
1960–69	1.10	1.15	1.00
1970–79	1.10	1.00	1.30
1980–85	1.43	1.50	1.61

Source: GSS, 1972–1985.

a. The years in which a cohort turned twenty.

b. "Professional or managerial" in U.S. census codes.

c. "Professional, managerial, clerical, and sales" in U.S. census codes.

does not mean that there were more Catholics in college than Protestants, but that Catholics were more likely than Protestants to attend college.

In the early decades of this century the ratio of Catholics to Protestants in the decision to go to college was approximately .70: Catholics were about 70 percent as likely to attend college as Protestants. In the 1930s and the 1940s, this ratio increased to about .90. During the 1950s, 1960s, and 1970s the Catholic college attendance rate caught up to and passed the white Protestant rate. In 1961, in the first NORC study of college graduates, Catholics were 25 percent of the population and 25 percent of the college graduates. By the first half of the 1980s Catholics were almost half again as likely to attend college as white Protestants (1.43). These data from GSS are confirmed by research done at the Higher Educational Research Institute (HERI) and UCLA. According to HERI data, Catholics accounted for 37 percent of college freshmen in 1984.

These data do not indicate a decline in white Protestant college attendance; nor do they mean that more Catholics go to college than Protestants. (Catholics, it will be remembered, are a quarter of the population, Protestants almost two-thirds.) Rather they mean an increase in the rate of Catholic college attendance relative to white Protestant college attendance. The proportion of young Catholics going to college has passed and exceeded the proportion of young white Protestants going to college.

Similar ratios are observable in terms of professional (professional or managerial) and white-collar careers. In the early part of this century Catholics were less likely than Protestants to achieve such career prestige. After the Second World War Catholics achieved parity. And in the present decade Catholics have surged ahead.

The dynamics of this social change are beyond the scope of this report. It suffices to say that one of the most notable religious changes in this century is that Catholics have achieved social and economic parity with white Protestants.

Table 7.2 presents annual family income for Jews, selected Protestant denominations, and Catholic ethnic groups under forty.

Table 7.2. Income by religion, denomination, and ethnicity among whites under forty, 1980–1984

Group	Annual family income ($)
Jewish	36,291
Italian Catholic	30,321
Irish Catholic	28,985
Polish Catholic	27,858
Presbyterian	27,513
Episcopalian	25,136
Lutheran	25,012
Methodist	23,910
German Catholic	23,785
Baptist	21,618
Hispanic Catholic	16,426

Source: Pooled data, GSS, 1980–1984.

The income figures represent the actual dollars in the year of the survey and thus do not take into account inflation in the last ten years. Hence they are not measures of absolute income today, but of relative income among the various groups.

The most affluent American denominational groups among those under forty were the Jews, the Episcopalians, the Presbyterians, and the Catholics. Among Catholic ethnic groups, Italian, Irish, and Polish Catholics under forty had a higher annual income than anyone but the Jews. The important point about these figures is not the marginal Catholic ethnic advantage over the two elite Protestant denominations, but the relative parity. Even if variables such as urban versus rural or northern versus southern residence are taken into account (which would surely increase the relative position of Lutherans and German Catholics), it would be clear that a Catholic ethnic background (unless it be Hispanic) is no longer a barrier to financial success in America. American white Catholics have achieved a rough economic parity with their Protestant counterparts.

Has this economic success had a political impact? More precisely, has the prediction, heard since Catholic migration to the suburbs began in the late 1940s, that Catholics would leave the Democratic party as they entered the middle class, been sustained?

Figure 7.1 shows that Protestant and Catholic voting for presidents in the eight presidential elections of 1952–1980 has varied greatly, depending on the candidates. The data show a disproportionate Catholic increase in Democratic voting in the Kennedy and Johnson years and a disproportionate though smaller and statistically significant decline in Catholic Democratic voting *relative to Protestant Democratic voting* in the Nixon years, but no statistically significant changes since then until 1980. (Preliminary data for the 1984 election indicate that although the majority of Catholics voted for President Reagan, the Catholic Democratic vote relative to the Protestant Democratic vote did not change.)

Everyone was more likely to vote Democratic in the Kennedy and Johnson years than in the Eisenhower years, but Catholics

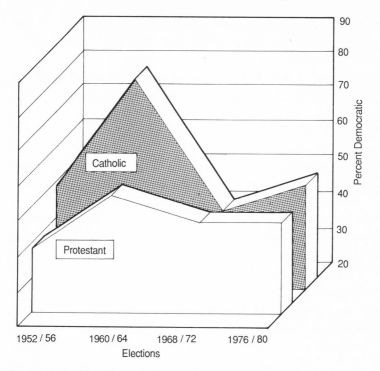

Figure 7.1. Presidential vote by denomination, 1952–1980 (combined elections) (SRC, national election years).

were most likely to vote Democratic. Everyone was less likely to vote Democratic during the Humphrey and McGovern years than during the early and middle 1960s, but Catholics were least likely to vote Democratic. In the Carter years the ebb and flow of Catholic presidential voting was no different from that of the American average.

This analysis accords with that of Paul Lopatto in his careful book *Religion and the Presidential Election* (1985). There were two religious elections in the last thirty years, he argues, in the sense that only twice was there a departure from the relative voting patterns of Catholics and Protestants: In 1960 Catholics voted disproportionately for John Kennedy (relative to their previous voting pattern) and Protestants voted disproportionately for Richard Nixon (relative to their previous voting patterns). In 1972 religiously "conservative" Protestants voted disproportionately for the Republican candidate (Nixon), and "liberal" Protestants disproportionately for the Democrat (McGovern), in both cases because the voters' political opinions on foreign and domestic policies (war and race) coincided with those of the candidates. The Catholics' defection from the Democrats in the 1972 election is more difficult to explain because, like the liberal Protestants (as Lopatto effectively shows), their political position was closer to the Democrats' than to the Republicans' (against the war and more tolerant racially). The Catholic change was candidate related rather than issue related.

Despite the introduction of the "religious issue" into political campaigns by the mass media, religion has not made a difference in voting patterns since 1972. Swings back and forth occur with equal momentum among both Catholics and Protestants. For all the public outcry over abortion in the 1984 election, for example, only 1 percent of Catholics in the *New York Times* exit survey thought it was the most important issue in the election, and only 4 percent thought it was one of the two most important issues (compared with 8 percent of Protestants).

Although Catholics abandoned the Democratic presidential candidate in 1972 and have been less than enthusiastic about his two successors, they have not deserted the Democratic party in either House or Senate races (Figures 7.2, 7.3). The data show an effect by year but not an effect by religion. In fact, in 1980 Catholics were more likely to vote for Democratic congressional candidates than they were in the 1950s. Social and economic success does not seem to have affected the Catholic propensity to send Democrats to the House and Senate in the last thirty years.

The Democratic party lost some adherents in the late 1960s and early 1970s (Figure 7.4), but that loss stopped in the mid-1970s. (It may have begun again in the Reagan years, but more

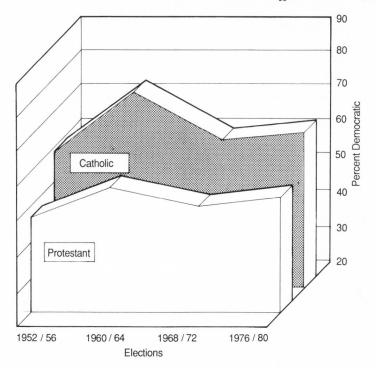

Figure 7.2. House vote by denomination in presidential years, 1952–1980 (combined elections) (SRC, national election years).

time will have to pass before we can make a reliable political assessment of that era.)

The data in Figure 7.4 (the one which in comparison with the graphs in Chapter 4 led Hout and me to consider the possible relationships between church attendance and political affiliation) show a decline in Democratic affiliation in both religious groups in 1968/1972 and a slightly higher (but statistically significant) decline among Catholics than among Protestants. The left wing of the party in those years, it appears, alienated some Catholics and some Protestants, but relatively speaking more Catholics than Protestants.

There was no further decline in Catholics' Democratic affilia-

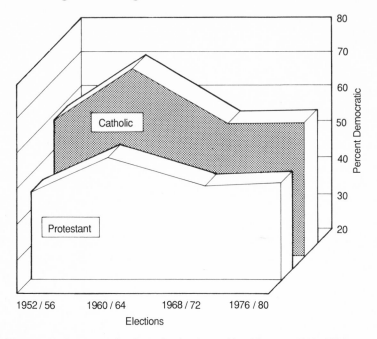

Figure 7.3. Senate vote by denomination in presidential years, 1952–1980
(combined elections) (SRC, national election years).

tion in 1976/1980, and the greater propensity of Catholics to identify as Democrats continues—diminished (like weekly church attendance) but still higher than that of Protestants. (The available 1984 data suggest that there may be a significantly disproportionate decline in Protestant affiliation with the Democratic party, but it is impossible to claim a "realignment" on the basis of one election.)

Strength of party affiliation, like regularity of church attendance, tends to increase with age for both Protestants and Catholics. (In 1974 Knoke and Hout demonstrated that there is not an important cohort effect here either.) In both groups the proportion who are pure independents does not change with age (Table 7.3), but among those who have affiliated there is a tendency with age for a drift toward "strong" affiliation. It would

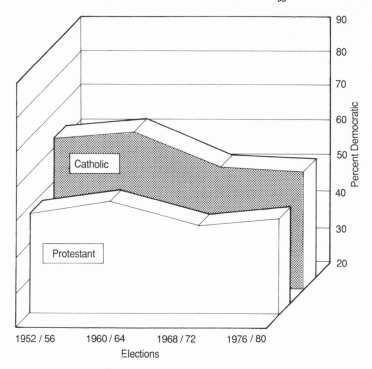

Figure 7.4. Democratic identification by denomination, 1952–1980 (combined elections) (SRC, national election years).

appear that in their late teens or early twenties most Americans decide to affiliate with a political party, and with a religious group through a decision to attend church. Once this decision has been made, there is little increase in the proportion of those who have chosen to be pure independents or "never" go to church. But among those who do affiliate there is a tendency for both strong affiliation and more regular church attendance.

The negative correlation between Catholicism and educational and career achievement not only has diminished to nonexistence in this century but has been replaced with a positive correlation. The positive correlation between Catholic and Democratic affiliation has also diminished, especially in the late 1960s and early

Table 7.3.   Life-cycle party affiliation of Protestants and Catholics, 1972–1985 (%)

	Protestant		Catholic	
Age	Strong party affiliation	"Independent"	Strong party affiliation	"Independent"
18–19	15	14	18	19
20–24	14	16	18	19
25–29	16	14	20	16
30–34	22	13	18	14
35–39	20	12	23	11
40–44	24	11	19	13
45–49	26	10	30	12
50–54	25	9	35	9
55–59	28	7	44	7
60–64	34	8	35	7
65–69	41	7	36	11
Over 70	40	8	36	9

Source: Pooled data, GSS, 1972–1985.
Note: "Independents" are those leaning to neither party.

1970s, but continues to exist—and the decline in the correlation seems to have stopped. Protestants are no longer more affluent than Catholics, but Catholics are still more Democratic than Protestants. Whether this continued Democratic affiliation indicates an increased conservatism in Catholic political and social attitudes will be the subject of the next chapter.

Chapter 8

Social and Sexual Attitudes

The decline in Catholics' affiliation with the Democratic party and in their propensity, even in Republican presidential years, to vote Democratic more than Protestants do raises the question whether Catholics are becoming more conservative. But to answer that question we must compare their political attitudes with those of other groups.

In his analysis of the 1984 presidential election, sociologist Seymour Martin Lipset observed that in terms of their political attitudes, Catholics continue to be to the right of Jews (who constitute 3 percent of Americans) and to the left of Protestants, (who constitute 60 percent of Americans).

The issue, then, is whether there has been a change in the relative position of the groups over time. Table 8.1 shows that from 1972 to 1985, the relative position of the three religious groups on the political spectrum has not changed much.

Catholics continue to be more concerned about the environment, health, and cities than are white Protestants (as these concerns are measured by feeling that more money should be spent on them.) They continue to be more likely to think that too much money is being spent on arms. In the early 1970s they were marginally less likely than Protestants to oppose the death penalty, and in the early 1980s marginally more likely because of a sharp Protestant decline in opposition to the death penalty. They continue to be more likely (by 14 percentage points) to favor gun control. Moreover, they are also more likely than white

Table 8.1. Political and social attitudes of white Catholics, Protestants, and Jews, 1972–1975 and 1982–1985 (%)

	1972–1975	1982–1985
"Too little spent on environment"		
Protestants	58	50
Catholics	67	60
Jews	83	67
"Too little spent on health"		
Protestants	59	54
Catholics	66	63
Jews	85	62
"Too little spent on urban problems"		
Protestants	49	42
Catholics	49	52
Jews	86	65
"Too little spent on education"		
Protestants	43	57
Catholics	50	59
Jews	72	74
"Too much spent on arms"		
Protestants	30	27
Catholics	39	38
Jews	61	64
Oppose capital punishment		
Protestants	29	18
Catholics	25	22
Jews	56	19
Support open housing ordinance		
Protestants	32	42
Catholics	36	52
Jews	46	52
Support busing		
Protestants	12	16
Catholics	14	24
Jews	21	12
Reject "Women unqualified for politics"		
Protestants	47	59
Catholics	54	67
Jews	73	84

Source: GSS, 1972–1975 and 1982–1985 (pooled surveys).

Protestants to reject racial segregation of neighborhoods and to support open housing laws (by a majority in the early 1980s). They continue to be more likely to support bussing (24 percent in 1985) and to reject the notion that women are not qualified for politics. Finally, in such matters as open housing ordinances, Catholics in the early 1980s were similar to Jews in their attitudes.

Among Protestant denominations (Table 8.2), Baptists and Methodists are in general the most conservative and Episcopalians

Table 8.2. Social and political attitudes of white Protestants, by denomination, 1972–1975 and 1982–1985 (%)

	1972–1975	1982–1985
Oppose capital punishment		
Baptist	29	18
Methodist	29	22
Lutheran	32	16
Presbyterian	32	17
Episcopalian	27	19
Other	30	22
No denomination	20	18
Support open housing ordinance		
Baptist	32	42
Methodist	32	40
Lutheran	30	38
Presbyterian	32	45
Episcopalian	47	52
Other	32	44
No denomination	34	49
Reject "Women unqualified for politics"		
Baptist	41	57
Methodist	43	61
Lutheran	54	63
Presbyterian	55	59
Episcopalian	61	83
Other	46	55
No denomination	53	61

Source: GSS, 1972–1975 and 1982–1985 (pooled surveys).

and Presbyterians the most liberal on the issues of capital punishment, open housing, and women in politics. However, generally they are not more liberal than Catholics.

If a measure of the importance of religion in a society is the
power of religious affiliation to influence political and social attitudes (either directly, through doctrinal or imaginative content,
or indirectly, through social and economic factors), there is no
indication in the GSS data that this importance has been eroded
in recent years. Since Catholics are generally believed to be more
conservative than liberal, no one has attempted to study the reason
for their greater liberalism. (In the next chapter I suggest that
the reason might be the shape of the Catholic religious
imagination.)

Whether there has been a sexual revolution in the last twenty
years or not is largely a question of terminology. That there has
been an increase in premarital sex and divorce since the early
1960s is beyond debate. Divorce rates have increased sharply in
the past decade—from 21 to 30 percent for Protestants, from 16
to 24 percent for Catholics. But it remains arguable whether
there has been a vast change in sexual practice or whether some
important modifications of the technology of fertility control have
simply made certain sexual practices either easier or less threatening than in the past.

A useful minimalist description of what has happened is that
the interaction between effective fertility control technology (especially the Pill) and a greater demand for women in the labor
force has given women greater economic and sexual freedom and
hence increased the premarital sex and divorce rates. Here we can
only consider certain indicators measured in the GSS since 1972:
attitudes toward premarital and extramarital sex, homosexuality,
divorce, and abortion. Table 8.3 includes Jewish attitudes for
comparative rather than descriptive purposes; that is, the data
cannot provide precise measures of Jewish attitudes or changes
through time but will enable us to say whether they are different
in statistically significant ways from gentile attitudes.

Table 8.3. Sexual attitudes of white Protestants, Catholics, and Jews, 1972–1975 and 1982–1985 (%)

	1972–1975	1982–1985
Premarital sex always wrong		
Protestants	38	34
Catholics	32	22
Jews	14	14
Premarital sex never wrong		
Protestants	25	36
Catholics	30	45
Jews	48	61
Extramarital sex always wrong		
Protestants	76	77
Catholics	74	71
Jews	39	46
Homosexuality always wrong		
Protestants	77	80
Catholics	71	69
Jews	32	45
Divorce laws should be easier		
Protestants	28	25
Catholics	27	23
Jews	51	34
Approve birth control information for teenagers		
Protestants	79	86
Catholics	79	87
Jews	91	99
Abortion should be available if there is danger to woman's health		
Protestants	91	90
Catholics	86	86
Jews	98	99
Abortion should be available if woman wants no more children		
Protestants	44	39
Catholics	35	37
Jews	85	82

Source: GSS, 1972–1975 and 1982–1985 (pooled surveys).

Both Catholics and Protestants were more likely in 1972 than in 1985 to think that premarital sex was always wrong and less likely to think that it was never wrong. At both times Jews were significantly more tolerant of premarital sex than gentiles. By 1985 Catholics were also significantly more tolerant than Protestants: 22 percent of Catholic respondents thought that it was always wrong and 45 percent of Catholics that it was never wrong, whereas 34 percent of Protestants believed it was always wrong and 36 percent believed it was never wrong.

Despite vigorous pressure from church leaders during the last decade and a half, then, Catholics were more likely than Protestants to be affected by the sexual revolution in their attitudes toward premarital sex. Both groups were also more likely in the mid-1980s than in the early 1970s to support the provision of birth control information to teenagers. Protestant opposition to sex education in schools declined from 22 percent to 16 percent, while Catholic opposition to sex education, ten points lower than Protestant opposition in 1972, remained at 12 percent in 1984. On the other hand, both Protestants and Catholics were less likely in 1984 to think that divorce laws should be made easier, perhaps because laws had already been eased in the intervening years.

Despite all the controversy about abortion, neither Catholics nor Protestants seem to have changed their opinions or to differ from one another on this issue since 1972. Majorities of both groups (more than nine-tenths) continued to approve of access to abortion if a mother's health was in danger, and approximately two-fifths of both groups approved of abortion if the woman simply did not want any more children.

Both groups' attitudes toward homosexuality and extramarital sex have changed slightly. Protestants have become marginally less tolerant of either behavior than they were in 1972, and Catholics are now marginally more tolerant than Protestants of homosexuality and extramarital sex. However, more than two-thirds of American Catholics and three-quarters of American Protestants continue to reject both forms of behavior.

Insofar as our data can measure it, the sexual revolution is not total and affects Catholics somewhat more than it does Protestants. Despite Pope John Paul II's attempt since 1980 to recall Catholics to the traditional sexual ethic of their church, there has been no observable impact on Catholic attitudes about abortion, birth control information for adolescents, and premarital sex during the half-decade. If anything, Catholic opinion has shifted marginally away from papal teaching.

Five propositions summarize the data in Table 8.3: (1) Both Protestant and Catholic attitudes on premarital sex have changed since 1972; (2) neither group has changed its opinion on extramarital sex or abortion; (3) the principal division on sexual matters continues to be between Jews and gentiles; (4) among gentiles, Catholics are now somewhat more sexually tolerant than Protestants; and (5) the Vatican's counteroffensive to promote the traditional Catholic social ethic has not (at least not yet) had an observable impact on Catholic attitudes.

The sociologist reports the attitudes that are and leaves to the ethicist the issue of what attitudes should be. Morality is not derived by head count, but neither can ethical reasoning ignore completely the data provided by head counters. Pope John Paul himself has said that in matters of marriage and sex, the married laity have a unique and indispensable contribution to make to the Church's understanding and that social research is a helpful way of measuring that experience if not the only way.

No reasonable sociologist could claim any more.

Despite the conventional wisdom, in political, social, and ethical attitudes Catholics tend to be more liberal than Protestants, and more conservative than Jews. Neither the counteroffensive of Pope John Paul nor their enhanced economic status has changed Catholics' position between the two other groups, although in the last decade Catholics have tended to shift disproportionately toward greater political and social liberalism and more sexual tolerance.

Chapter 9

Religious Images

The "religious indicators" analyzed in the previous chapters are useful measures of religious behavior. But from the viewpoint of the sociologist they suffer from two major weaknesses: (1) they do not measure the basic orientation of the human personality toward the ultimate (or the Ultimate), which many definitions of religion take to be the essential component of religion; and (2) they have little predictive power: frequent church attendance, for example, does not correlate with other measures of human attitudes and activity. This chapter suggests a new battery of religious questions for future social indicator research on religion. By focusing on the religious imagination, these questions satisfy the demands of theories which define religion as a system of symbols which provide ultimate meaning for life (of which such indicators as church attendance are poor and indirect measures), correlate more strongly than the traditional religious indicators with other varieties of attitudes and behavior, and help to explain the differences between Protestants and Catholics in social and political attitudes.

Taking my lead from such scholars of religion as William James (1902), who emphasized the importance of religious experience, Rudolph Otto (1952), who contended that religion originates in the experience of the holy, and Clifford Geertz (1966), who defines religion as a set of symbols which purport uniquely to explain the meaning of life and serve as templates for responding to and shaping the experience of life, I have contended elsewhere (Greeley, 1978) that religion begins with experiences which renew human hope, that these experiences are stored in the memory as symbols—special memory traces which act as templates for life's ultimate problems—and that they are shared with others through stories designed to recall from their memories traces of similar experiences. Our overarching religious tradition provides the repertoire of images with symbolic potential which antecedently dispose us for hope renewal experiences, shape the experience itself, act as "storage containers" which hold the memory of that experience, and facilitate the storytelling by which we share our hope renewal experiences with others who possess the traditional images in common with us.

For example: Discouraged and depressed with the futility of life, I wait for an endlessly delayed flight in December at Chicago's O'Hare Airport. I see a young mother holding her baby with passionate and protective adoration. In the beauty of that instant recognition of grounds for hope, my confidence in the purpose of life is revitalized and renewed. The friends who meet me at the end of the plane flight are astonished at my good spirits. Today, I tell them by way of explanation, I met a madonna.

The madonna image, lurking in my memory on the threshold of consciousness, especially in December, disposes me to experience renewal in the presence of a mother with a child, shapes that actual experience, provides a "pigeonhole" into which I can insert my new experience, and becomes a shared symbol with which I can explain my unusual (after plane flights) cheerfulness to my friends. If someone should preach a Christmas homily about the madonna, I remember both images—Bethlehem and O'Hare—and "correlate" them; each gives emotional vitality and resonance to the other. Catechisms, creeds, doctrines, philosophy, and theology—essential reflection on and criticism of the moments of raw religious experience—all come later. The origin and raw power of experience reside in life-explaining experiences. Religion is a meaning-bestowing story before it becomes anything else.

In the story which each one of us is writing of our life, the religious symbols—the network of traces of decisive hope renewal experiences—are the basic subplot.

In the film *All That Jazz,* director Bob Fosse shares with us the hope renewal which occurred when he briefly "died" during heart surgery and discovered that death was not evil or ugly but rather gentle and loving—like his wife or his mistress or, especially, his daughter. Could, he asks in a paraphrase of the crucial religious question, death be God and God be like a loving woman?

If such a model of religion (and it is by no means presented here as an exclusive model) has value, it follows that one of the tasks of the sociologist of religion is to develop measures of the religious imagination which, if the theory is correct and the measures sensitive, ought to be moderately successful predictors of other attitudes and behaviors—which the traditional social indicators reported on in earlier chapters are not.

After considerable experimentation, NORC has included in the GSS since 1984 a religious imagination question which presents choices between six pairs of "traditional" versus "modern" or perhaps "distant" versus "intimate" images of God. Because this measure has been used for such a short time, it cannot reveal any trends; but it may prove to be a very useful indicator in the future.

> There are many different ways of picturing God. On a scale of 1-7 where would you place yourself between the two contrasting images:
>
> Mother . . . . . Father
> Master . . . . . Spouse
> Judge . . . . . Lover
> Friend . . . . . King
> Creator . . . . . Healer
> Redeemer . . . . . Liberator

Only 7 percent of respondents are unable to answer these items. As Table 9.1 shows, the more intimate and intense images—

Table 9.1. Images of God, 1985–1987 (% choosing specified image or midpoint between opposed images)

Image	%
Mother	24
Spouse	32
Lover	50
Friend	71
Healer	61
Liberator	50

Source: GSS, 1985–1987 (pooled surveys).

Mother and Spouse (which have a solid basis in the Christian and Jewish traditions)—are less popular than slightly less intense intimate images such as Lover, Friend, Healer, and Liberator. Nonetheless, 24 percent of respondents picture God as at least halfway between Mother and Father (8 percent incline to picture God as Mother), and 32 percent picture Her/Him as at least halfway between Master and Spouse (13 percent incline to picture God as Spouse). None of the responses correlates with age, sex, or education.

If intimate and intense images of a relationship with God are the key theme in the story of a person's life, then these images should shape a life in which there is greater sympathy and compassion for other humans. Thus we would predict that those who choose an image of God which is halfway between Mother and Father—and thus an androgynous image—would be more liberal on issues such as equality for women and blacks, the death penalty, and perhaps even in their presidential voting.

Table 9.2 sustains the prediction. Those who think of God at least as both Mother and Father are 17 percentage points more likely to disagree with the statement "Most men are better suited to politics than are most women." Although the majority of Americans now support the death penalty, those who have androgynous images of God are half again as likely as their opposites

Table 9.2.   Political attitudes and behavior by image of God as Mother[a] or Father (%)

	Image of God	
Attitude/behavior	Mother[a]	Father
Oppose death penalty	27	18[b]
Women unsuited to politics	78	61[b]
Voted for Reagan	47	65[b]
Blacks ought not to push (disagree)	45	38[b]

Source: GSS, 1985–1987 (pooled surveys).

a. Mother or midpoint.

b. Statistically significant difference.

to disapprove of capital punishment (27 versus 18 percent). Forty-five percent of them, in contrast to 38 percent of those whose image of God is predominantly male, reject the opinion that "Blacks shouldn't push themselves where they are not wanted." All the differences are statistically significant. One's picture of God, in other words, has considerable influence on one's picture of the world.

People's images of God even affect their voting behavior: those who picture God as both Father and Mother or more as Mother than as Father were 18 percentage points less likely to have voted for Ronald Reagan in 1984. If indeed all Americans were on the Mother end of the Mother–Father continuum, Walter Mondale would today be president of the United States.

Nor is this influence merely a matter of an underlying dimension of "liberalism" which produces more "enlightened" attitudes toward both God and world. Within each category of self-described political views, statistically significant relationships persist in eight of the twelve comparisons in Table 9.3. Thirty-six percent of self-described liberals who had an image of God as Father voted for Reagan, compared with only 19 percent of those who had an androgynous image. Among moderates, the percentages were 64 and 51, respectively. Only among conservatives

Table 9.3. Political orientation by self-described political stance and image of God as Mother[a] or Father, 1985–1987 (%)

Self-description/ image of God	Voted for Reagan	Women unfit for politics (disagree)	Oppose death penalty	Blacks ought not to push (disagree)
Liberal				
Mother[a]	19	77	38	60
Father	36[b]	63[b]	25[b]	45[b]
Moderate				
Mother[a]	51	68	24	33
Father	64[b]	59[b]	17[b]	39
Conservative				
Mother[a]	75	67	18	39
Father	79	50[b]	15	33

Source: GSS, 1985–1987 (pooled surveys).

a. Mother or midpoint.

b. Statistically significant.

did image of God not have a statistically significant effect on presidential voting behavior. However, even among self-described conservatives, image of God made a statistically significant difference in their view of the role of women in politics. Thus, one's image of God affects (especially) conservative attitudes toward women and liberal and moderate attitudes toward blacks, capital punishment, and presidential candidates.

If the images one has of God are a surrogate for psychological or attitudinal liberalism, they are a remarkably effective and easy-to-administer measure. A composite measure consisting of presidential voting and attitudes toward civil liberties, blacks, and the death penalty correlates with a composite measure made up of Mother/Father, Master/Spouse, Judge/Lover, and Friend/King at .18. When five other measures of liberalism—political, economic (more government help for the poor), religious (literal truth of the Bible), social (legalization of marijuana), and abortion (on demand)—are added to a regression equation, the correlation falls to .15. Religious imagery, in other words, makes an important contribution in its own right and not as a substitute for various dimensions of liberalism (insofar as we can measure these dimensions).

It is also the only religious measure currently available which seems to relate to political and social attitudes (Table 9.4). Prayer, self-described religious intensity, church attendance, and confidence in religious leaders have no significant impact on the political factor described in the previous paragraph.

Moreover, this correlation is stronger for Catholics than for Protestants and reduces, together with the effect of disproportionate Protestant representation in the South, the relationship between Catholicism and political liberalism (as measured by the factor described above) to statistical insignificance (Table 9.5). The different religious imagery of Catholics contributes to their different political attitudes and behavior.

But this difference is concentrated entirely among Catholics under forty-five. Protestants both under and over forty-five and Catholics over forty-five have identical mean scores on the religious imagery factor. Hence, it is possible to surmise that the religious images of Catholics under forty-five represent a cohort

Table 9.4. Correlation between image measure and attitude scale compared with other religious measures, 1985–1987

	Protestants	Catholics
Images[a]	.12[b]	.20[b]
Prayer	.05	.05
Strength of religion	.00	.02
Attendance	.00	.03
Confidence in religious leaders	.01	.01

Source: GSS, 1985–1987.

Note: Scale composed of attitudes on race, death penalty, poverty, civil liberties, and voting in presidential election.

a. Scale in direction of God as Mother, Lover, Spouse, and Friend.

b. Statistically significant.

Table 9.5.   Liberalism of Catholics by images and region (% of standard deviation difference between Protestants and Catholics)

Raw difference	29
Net of region	21
Net of region and images of God as Mother, Lover, Friend, Spouse	15[a]

Source: Greeley, based on GSS, 1984.

Note: Scale composed of attitudes on race, death penalty, poverty, civil liberties, and voting in presidential election.

a. Not statistically significant.

change and not a life-cycle change, perhaps as a result of the influence of the Second Vatican Council, or perhaps even as a result of turning to a sympathetic God from an unsympathetic ecclesiastical leadership on the birth control issue. It would be ironic if in the crisis of personal decision making on the subject of birth control, many Catholics developed images of God more in keeping with the Catholic tradition. But such explanations must remain merely speculative for now. Only time will reveal whether religious image measures which apparently correlate with other dimensions of human life more powerfully than to the traditional devotional measures are as invariant as the devotional measures seem to be.

In addition to an instrument on images of God, NORC has developed two other sets of symbol measures which attempt to tap basic religious orientations—pictures of life after death and images of the goodness of the world.

People picture life after death in many different ways. We'd like to know how you think of life after death. Here is a card with sets of contrasting images. On a scale of 1–7 where would you place your image of life after death . . .

(d) A pale, shadowy form of life, hardly life at all / a life of complete fulfillment, spiritual and physical.

And:

People have different images of the world and human nature.
We'd like to know the kinds of images you have.
Here is a card with sets of contrasting images. On a scale of 1–
7 where would you place your image of the world and human
nature between the two contrasting images . . .
(d) Human nature is basically good. / Human nature is funda-
mentally perverse and corrupt.

Two other variables that are affected by the religious images
of the respondent are psychological well-being (as measured by
a simple question asking whether the respondent is "very" happy,
"pretty" happy, or "not too" happy) and attitudes toward premarital sex. Both variables correlate with images of God as Lover
instead of as Judge and of life after death as "a life of complete
fulfillment, spiritual and physical" rather than "a pale, shadowy
form of life, hardly life at all."

Forty-seven percent of Protestants who describe themselves as
"very happy" think of God as Lover (Table 9.6), compared with
30 percent of Protestants who think of God as Judge. The differences among Catholics are not statistically significant. Protestants who report high morale are also more likely to view life
after death as an existence of fulfillment (37 percent) rather than
as a "pale, shadowy life" (24 percent). The differences persist in
all Protestant denominations, among those who go to church
regularly and those who do not, and among those who are strong
religious identifiers and those who are not. However, there is
little difference in these perceptions among Catholics who de-

Table 9.6. Protestants and Catholics self-described as "very happy," by
religious images, 1985–1987 (%)

Image of God/afterlife	Protestant	Catholic
God as Judge	30	36
God as Lover	47	37
Afterlife "pale"	24	36
Afterlife fulfilling	37	35

Source: GSS, 1985–1987 (pooled surveys).

scribe themselves as "very happy." Regardless of denomination and devotion, then, the picture of God as Lover and of the hereafter as a place of fulfillment does correlate with psychological well-being. The images are an independent religious factor with a powerful influence on a morale measure that is not normally affected so strongly by predictor variables.

The same finding applies to the relationship between these two measures and attitudes toward premarital sex (Table 9.7). Forty-nine percent of those who picture God as Lover think premarital sex is "always wrong," in contrast to 33 percent of those who think of God as Judge. Love more than fear of the Judge thus seems to be a motivation for disapproval of premarital sex—and in this case for both Protestants and Catholics at the level of statistical significance. An image of the hereafter as fulfilling has the same considerable impact on sexual attitudes at the level of statistical significance for both Protestants and Catholics. These correlations also persist in all denominational and devotional groups, from the most orthodox (Baptists) to the least orthodox (Episcopalians and Presbyterians). People's images of God and the hereafter influence their morale and their attitude on premarital sex whatever their denomination. For example, Episcopalians who think of life after death as fulfilling are more likely (26 percent) to reject premarital sex than are Catholics (13 percent) and Methodists (19 percent) who do not think of the hereafter as fulfilling.

Both variables operate independently, as Table 9.8 demon-

Table 9.7. Protestants and Catholics viewing premarital sex as "always wrong," by religious images, 1985–1987 (%)

Image of God/afterlife	Protestant	Catholic
God as Judge	33	18
God as Lover	49	37
Afterlife "pale"	21	13
Afterlife fulfilling	45	29

Source: GSS, 1985–1987 (pooled surveys).

Table 9.8.   Attitudes by images of God and afterlife, 1985–1987 (%)

	God as Judge	God as Lover[a]
Self-described "very happy"		
Afterlife "pale"	27	28
Afterlife fulfilling	33[b]	50[b]
Premarital sex "always wrong"		
Afterlife "pale"	18	12[c]
Afterlife fulfilling	37[b]	60[b]

Source: GSS, 1985–1987 (pooled surveys).

a. 7 on a scale of 1–7.

b. Row and column differences statistically significant.

c. Column difference statistically significant.

strates. Only in the first row of the table are the differences (by row and by column) not statistically significant. The greatest opposition to premarital sex and the greatest level of psychological well-being are to be found among those who picture God as Lover and the hereafter as a life of fulfillment. Half of those with these two benign images are "very happy," in contrast to a little more than a quarter of those who have neither image. And three-fifths of those with these images think that premarital sex is wrong, in contrast to 18 percent of those who lack both images. These results hold even when denominational background and religious devotion are held constant.

People's views of human nature also have a statistically significant impact on their attitudes about the role of women, race, and capital punishment (Table 9.9). The more benign one's view of human nature, the more tolerant one is likely to be.

Religious image items not only are useful as predictor variables; they also help the researcher to cope with complex problems on matters related to religion, such as the experience of contact with the dead.

In 1985 a group of medical researchers (specializing in family practice) reported a strikingly high incidence of "hallucinations" in which widows experience contact with their dead spouse (Olson

Table 9.9.   Social attitudes by view of human nature, 1985–1987 (%)

Social attitude	View of human nature	
	Basically good	Perverse
Women should stay home	24[a]	39
Oppose capital punishment	21[a]	14
Blacks should not push (disagree)	41[a]	35

Source: GSS, 1985–1987 (pooled surveys).
a. Statistically significant difference.

et al., 1985). The interviews on which the report was based were conducted in nursing homes and do not represent a probability sample of the American population. However, it was possible, using data collected in the 1984 GSS, to attempt a national probability replication of the medical researchers' work and to develop an explanatory model which would account for the higher incidence of such "contacts with the dead" (a term I prefer to "hallucination") among those who have lost husbands or wives—two-thirds versus 42 percent in the general population.

Forty-two percent of the 1,445 respondents reported contact with the dead; 41 percent of those who were not widowed, and 53 percent of the widowed (a statistically significant difference). Of the 149 widowed, 129 were women and 20 were men. The proportion of widows reporting contact with the dead "at least once or twice" was 64 percent, virtually the same as that recorded by Olson and his colleagues. Thus it appears that the incidence of contact with the dead reported in the nursing home survey is not substantially different from the incidence in the general population.

That almost two-thirds of the widows in the American population have had some contact with a dead person (presumably their spouse) is perhaps less surprising than the fact that two-fifths of the population who are not widowed also report such contact.

A "contact with the dead" experience correlates with age at a statistically significant level. Nonetheless, 38 percent of those in their teens and 40 percent of those in their twenties have also had such experiences.

The model developed for the present analysis assumes that religion might be involved in accounting for the disproportion of "contact" with the dead among the widowed. Religion, after all, purports to explain the ultimate purposes and the final tragedies of life. It is to religion that many men and women turn in times of grief. Might it not be that in attempting to resolve the grief of a tragic loss many people develop a religious intensity that disposes them to such encounters—whether real or imaginary, the social scientist cannot say—with the deceased spouse?

Moreover, since it is known that religious devotion correlates with age and the widowed tend to be older than the rest of the population, might it not be that the positive correlation between being widowed and contact with the dead can be accounted for by age and by higher levels of religious intensity or devotion?

Figure 9.1 presents such a model graphically. It proposes five significant relationships among the four variables "widowed," "age," "religion," and "contact." If the model can be fitted to

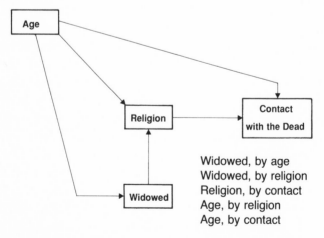

Widowed, by age
Widowed, by religion
Religion, by contact
Age, by religion
Age, by contact

Figure 9.1. Model for explaining contact with the dead among widowed.

the data as it stands, without a direct relationship between "widowed" and "contact," then we cannot reject a model which accounts for the disproportionate experience of contact with the dead among the widowed by a combination of age and religion.

Contact with the dead, perhaps not surprisingly, does correlate, and significantly, with a number of different measures of religious behavior. It is more likely to occur among those who believe in life after death—although 30 percent of those who do not believe in life after death still report having "felt as though I was really in touch with someone who had died"—a finding which surely should be a challenge to any social scientist exploring the incidence and prevalence of paranormal experiences in the American population.

Those who pray frequently and those who imagine God as Lover are more likely to have such experiences than those who do not pray frequently and those who imagine God as Judge. Finally, those who have had more than one experience of the other three kinds of psychic phenomena—déja vu, extrasensory perception, and clairvoyance—are almost twice as likely to report contact with the dead as those who have had only one such experience or less.

Six log linear models based on Figure 9.1 were fitted to the data. Estimates were made of the distribution of respondents for each of these models. The actual distributions of the data were compared with the estimated (or hypothesized) distribution.

Table 9.10 indicates that when church attendance, prayer, psychic experiences, or belief in life after death is inserted in the "religion" slot in the model in Figure 9.1, the observed distribution does differ significantly from the hypothesized distribution and therefore explanatory models containing each one of these variables can safely be rejected. Neither the religious commitment nor the religious imagination items, however, when placed in the "religion" slot, can be rejected. Since the chi-square is lower for the religious imagination item, a model which seeks to explain the higher incidence of contact with the dead among the widowed

Table 9.10. Explanatory models for "Contact with the dead" experiences among widowed

Variable	Chi-square	D.F.	p =
Church attendance	41.05	26	.03
Prayer	39.34	26	.04
Psychic experiences	31.72	26	.06
Belief in life after death	31.02	26	.07
Religious commitment	30.85	26	.16
God as Lover/Judge	28.62	26	.33

"Contact with the dead" by image of God (percent reporting experience)

	Image of God	
	Lover	*Judge*
Widowed	73	40
Not widowed	46	49

in terms of a combination of age and religious imagination becomes the preferred model.

The relationship between the image of God as Lover and contact with the dead for those who are widowed is nicely illustrated in the crosstabulation in the lower part of Table 9.10. The image of God as Lover does not increase the probability of an experience of contact with the dead for those who are not widowed, but it does for those who are. Those who imagine God as Lover are 33 percentage points more likely to report a contact experience.

The larger question of why so many Americans report contact with the dead has not been solved, but the smaller question of why the widowed are more likely than others to report it seems, tentatively at least, to be explained by their age and by a disproportionate tendency to imagine God as Lover instead of as Judge.

Or so it seems.

Figure 9.1 assumes that the flow of causality moves from left to right, from "widowed" to "religion" (image of God as Lover instead of as Judge) to "contact with the dead." But there is no absolute necessity for the path to flow in this direction. Might

not the final step—a relationship between religion (the image of
God as Lover) and the experience of contact with the dead—flow
in the opposite direction, from right to left? Might not a bereaved
person first experience contact with the dead and then, as a result
of such an experience, shift upward on the Judge/Lover scale?
Logically, at any rate, if not metaphysically or theologically, such
a possibility cannot be rejected.

There is in principle a way of deciding the issue. If a religious
imagination scale could be administered to a sample of widowed
persons shortly after the death of the spouse and then subsequently
at periodic intervals administered again with other questions about
how the respondent was coping with loss and about possible
contact with the dead, we might be able to speak with greater
confidence about the causal flow in the upper path of the chart
in Figure 9.1.

But even to fantasize about such research is to understand how
extraordinarily complex the issues involved in such matters really
are. In the absence of such an elaborate, not to say virtually
impossible, experiment, we can at least ask whether the findings
reported in this analysis can be replicated in another bereaved
population where the grief, however intense it might be, might
not normally be so powerful as the grief over the loss of a spouse.

The 1984 GSS also asked whether respondents had lost a mother,
a father, a child, or a sibling at various times in their lives. For
the purposes of analysis here, the population was divided into
two groups on each of these questions: those who had experienced
such a loss within the last five years and those who either had
never lost a sibling or had done so more than five years ago. In
each of the cases, those who have suffered the loss are more likely
to report a contact experience than those who have not, but the
only statistically significant difference is for those who have lost
a sibling in recent years. The analytic question then becomes
whether the same model that accounted for the higher incidence
of contact with the dead among widows and widowers will also
explain the higher incidence among those who have lost siblings

(only 15 percent of the widowed reported a death of a sibling in the last five years). If one distributes a hypothesized population in such a fashion that age and image of God as Lover account for the relationship between the loss of a sibling and contact with the dead, how will such a hypothesized distribution relate to the actual distribution of respondents?

As Table 9.11 shows, the proposition that the same model explains contact with a sibling and contact with a spouse cannot be rejected: the chi-square is 27.21 with 23 degrees of freedom and a probability of .25. In both cases, then, age and religious imagery account for the differences. That the loss of a sibling normally would not cause as much grief as the loss of the spouse does not seem to matter.

Why sibling and spouse and not parent or child? Perhaps because sibling and spouse are part of one's own generation and have, in the ordinary course of events, shared life with the self longer than either a parent or a child.

Where does this finding leave us on the intricate question of the direction of the causal flow on the final step of the upper path in our analytic model? Although the death of a sibling is surely a tragic experience, it does not seem likely to force a person to

Table 9.11. Explanatory model for "contact with the dead" experiences among those whose sibling has died

Variable	Chi-square	D.F.	P =
Judge/Lover	27.21	23	.2

"Contact with the dead" by loss of sibling and image of God (percent reporting experience)

	Image of God	
	Lover	*Judge*
Loss of sibling in last 5 years	100[a]	54
No loss of sibling or loss more than 5 years ago	44	40

a. N = 5.

fall back on religious beliefs and to revise these beliefs more or less permanently in the direction of a more intense relationship with God as Lover. Or if sibling death does lead to such image modification, it would presumably not exercise quite the same power as the loss of a spouse.

Obviously, we must be cautious in suggesting even a tentative answer to the question, but it would seem that the replication of the "spouse loss" phenomenon in the "sibling loss" situation might inch us a little in the direction of a contact> religion causal flow while still leaning preponderantly in the direction of a religion> contact flow. Despite an inclination to believe that it is the changing religious imagery which produces a propensity to experience contact with the dead, the replication in the sibling loss phenomenon must cause us to consider more seriously that it is the actual contact which affects the religious imagination and not vice versa—or at least that there is an intricate reciprocal flow between the two phenomena.

To consider seriously the possibility that an experience of being in touch with a person who is dead might influence the bereaved person to hold a more benign view of God—and presumably of the purposes of human life—is to make no suggestions at all about the "reality" of such experiences. As one of the founding fathers of modern sociology, W. I. Thomas, remarked, if something is defined as real, that definition itself becomes a reality to be studied.

Religious imagination items are more powerful predictors of human attitudes and behavior than most other religious measures; they are therefore potentially useful tools for future explorations of the relation between religious, social, and political behavior.

Chapter 10

American Religion, Civil and Uncivil

Four of the figures in this book summarize the basic findings about change in American religion. Figure 2.1 shows that acceptance of the literal interpretation of the Bible has declined, but only among Catholics. Figure 3.3 portrays the decline in the proportion of Protestants remaining in the mainline churches. Figure 4.1 summarizes the decline in church attendance among Catholics, which ended in 1975. Figure 6.2 shows the decline in contributions among Catholics.

The first change, the result of the impact of the Second Vatican Council's revision of Catholic teaching about the Bible on younger and college-educated Catholics (and especially younger college-educated Catholics), is not a departure from Catholic orthodoxy. The third change has apparently stopped, with loyalty counteracting the impact of the birth control encyclical. We do not know whether the fourth change will also be terminated by loyalty.

The second change is real enough, especially rapid among more recent cohorts, and undeniably threatening to the mainline denominations, especially to the Methodists. It does not, however, represent a change in Protestant devotion or practice, but rather a shift in the distribution of membership to match the devotional aspirations of congregants. It is nonetheless the only continuing major change in American religion that we have been able to document.

With the exception of this shifting of denominational affiliations, Protestantism has not changed in the last half-century. Catholicism has changed, but not much, and the change is over.

As they stand those two sentences of summary seem absurd. Protestantism has experienced the rise and fall of neoorthodoxy, the death and rebirth of the social gospel, migration from farm and small town to the city, the appearance of the electronic evangelist, the surge (or rediscovery) of fundamentalism and evangelicalism, the musical chairs of various denominational mergers, social and political conflict between activist clergy and conservative laity, the clerically launched and led civil rights movement, renewed controversy between literalist and nonliteralist interpretation of scripture, and the endless battle between science and religion.

Catholicism has experienced the twin transformation of the *embourgeoisement* of the children of immigrants and the *aggiornamento* of Vatican II. Its people have moved from the immigrant city to the professional suburbs, from unquestioning loyalty to frequently contentious independence, from Latin to English, from the Counter-Reformation to the ecumenical age, from pious and docile nuns to vocal supporters of the ordination of women, from the *Baltimore Catechism* to the Charismatic Renewal. Priests and nuns have left the active ministry by the thousands; others have become involved in radical political and social movements, some of them with Marxist tones; still others have doffed distinctive garb, insist on being called by first names, and instead of pretending that they have no personal problems, insist that their problems become the topic of constant conversation. Non-Catholic students flock to parochial grammar schools, Liberation Theology is taught in Catholic high schools, and professed atheists hold chairs of theology in Catholic universities.

How is it possible to argue that there has been no change in Protestantism and only minor change in Catholicism?

There are two possible responses to the question. One is to inquire whether there is as much change as meets the eye in the descriptions of the previous paragraphs insofar as it affects the daily religious life and faith of ordinary Catholic and Protestant laity. Is not the "changing church" a concern of the clergy, the lay elites, and the denominational journals of opinion rather than of typical congregants? Is not the "changing church" model an example of the future shock fallacy, which assumes that changes in technology and environment must change the fundamental dimensions of human life? Have not church members through the years shown remarkable skill in drawing from their faith what they want and need regardless of current organizational and theological fashions among their elites?

Priests on picket lines are news; but is there any reason to think that such activity has more than a peripheral effect on the religious life of Catholics? The protests of Catholic activists during the Vietnam war are frequently alleged to have turned the Catholic laity from hawks to doves, but survey data show that Catholics were always more dovish than typical white Americans, that their turn against the war antedated the Catholic peace movement, and that after each major public antiwar demonstration, there was an increase in support for the Nixon administration's conduct of the war. Are Catholics more likely than Protestants to oppose nuclear arms because of a pastoral letter by the American hierarchy? Or is the letter itself a result of lay concern? The survey data in this book show that Catholics were more likely to think that too much money was being spent on weapons ten years ago, long before the pastoral letter.

In other words, the ecclesiastical changes so widely publicized in the mass media may in fact have little effect on the religious life of individuals, families, and local communities. Such an effect needs to be proved, not assumed.

A second response is to concede the fact and the importance of the changes in American Christianity, and then add that social indicator research cannot hope to describe all the aspects of a phenomenon but only those for which there exist time-series data. Social indicators are at best a skeleton of a body politic or a body religious, an incomplete trajectory, an outline, a sketch. They represent truth as far as they go, but not, surely, the whole truth.

The second response is of course merely a less contentious version of the first. A little less explicitly than the first it says,

"Give us an operational measure of religious change and we'll try to find data to test it. Until then we must stand by the data we have; and these indicate that nothing much has changed."

Of the five models proposed in the first chapter, the secularization model fits only sexual ethics (and only some aspects of sexual ethics) and belief in literal interpretation of the Bible. Even the latter change is confined to younger and better-educated Catholics and represents a shift to a position which is, if anything, more orthodox for Catholics than strict literalism.

The kind of revivals predicted by the cyclic theory are certainly to be found in the AIPO question about the influence of religion in society, but the meaning of such an indicator is obscure; it may merely tell us that a lot of respondents see small fluctuations in religious influence, and it almost certainly represents a judgment about society and not about personal religious conviction. There may also be a revival of prayer and religious experience, although even at the presumed low points in such activities half of Americans prayed every day and one out of three had had at least a single intense religious experience. Interreligious attitudes, as measured by the SRC feeling thermometers, have fluctuated greatly during the years for which we have data, but there is no discernible pattern in such movement, and the relative positions of Protestants, Catholics, and Jews remain stable—with Catholics the losers in the tradeoff of warm feelings.

The episodic shock model seems to apply to Catholic church attendance rates, which fell sharply from 1969 to 1975 but have leveled off since. The decline was caused by the birth control encyclical, the stability by an underlying loyalty to the church.

Bible reading has increased over the last century, prayer may have increased in the last fifteen years, and certainly there is greater willingness to report ecstatic and paranormal experiences. So there is some confirmation for the increase of religion model which was noted at the beginning as a logical fifth possibility.

But most of the other social indicators discussed in the previous chapters best fit—sometimes with minor adjustments—the stability model. There has been no discernible change in belief in God, the divinity of Jesus, life after death, the existence of heaven, and divine influence on the Bible. The pattern of denominational affiliations has not changed (save for a possible decline in Methodism), nor have the propensities to become a church "member" and to belong to a church-affiliated voluntary organization (which still have the largest American organizational membership). The self-professed "strength" of religious affiliation has not changed, and this strength is proved by the fact that even among the most unreligious age group—those in their early twenties—half the Christians in the United States are inside a church at least once a month.

The position of the three major religious groups on the political spectrum has not changed: Protestants are still more likely to be Republican, Jews and Catholics more likely to be Democratic (with a decline in Democratic affiliation in the early 1970s which was marginally greater among Catholics than among Protestants). Jews are more likely to be liberal on political issues, Protestants to be conservative, and Catholics to be in the middle but to the left on the national averages and perhaps tilting somewhat more in the liberal direction during the last decade—despite their rapid movement up the social and economic ladder.

Basic doctrines, church attendance, prayer, organizational affiliation and activity, religious experience, location on the political spectrum—are not these indicators, superficial and naive as they might seem, at least a rough measure of the basic condition of religion in America? If they have not changed, is there not reason to assert that there is a certain long-term stability in American religious behavior whatever important changes might also be occurring? Is there not even more reason to assert that the secularization model, which is the conventional wisdom of many elite Americans, is unsupported by the available social indicators? Is it not true, then, that those who argue for or assume secularization now must labor under the burden of finding evidence to sustain their position?

Theodore Caplow and his colleagues, in their 1983 study of the religion of "Middletown" (Muncie, Indiana, first studied by Robert and Helen Lynd in 1924), note that in the late 1970s and early 1980s Middletown's religion had not changed on eleven major indicators for which there were measures at the beginning and the end of the sixty-year period:

> If secularization is a shrinkage of the religious sector in relation to other sectors of society . . . then it ought to produce some or all of the following indications: (1) a decline in the number of churches per capita of the population, (2) a decline in proportion of the population attending church services, (3) a decline in the proportion of rites of passage held under religious auspices (for example, declining ratios of religious to civil marriages and of religious to secular funerals), (4) a decline in religious endogamy, (5) a decline in the proportion of the labor force engaged in religious activity, (6) a decline in the proportion of income devoted to the support of religion, (7) a decline in the ratio of religious to non-religious literature, (8) a decline in the attention given to religion in the mass media, (9) a drift toward less emotional forms of participation in religious services, (10) a dwindling of new sects and of new movements in existing churches, and (11) an increase in attention paid to secular topics in sermons and liturgy. (Caplow et al., 1983, p. 34)

Though acknowledging that religion has changed greatly in Middletown since the 1920s, Caplow found no support for any of the eleven hypotheses (ibid., pp. 34–45). Muncie, Indiana, is the nation writ small in terms of the indicators analyzed in the previous chapters—a place of remarkable continuity in religious behavior.

Why, it is often asked by those who are prepared to accept the data gathered by researchers such as Caplow, is the United States so different from Europe, where "secularization" is so much further advanced? I suggest that if Europe is indeed secularized, then a consideration of religious practice in the rest of the world indicates that Europe, not the United States, is unique. Religion has lost none of its power in the Third World, despite the energies which we group under the label "modernization." Indeed the nonwestern religions all seem to be undergoing dramatic revivals. From a global perspective, the apparent failure of Christianity in some countries in Europe is the deviant case, not the norm, a fact which orthodox sociology—based as it is on the work of three great theorists of secularization (Karl Marx, Emile Durkheim, and Max Weber)—is most reluctant to admit.

In certain academic, journalistic, and religious circles, the response to the obvious sustained religiosity of Americans in comparison with the behavior of Western Europeans is to question the authenticity of the American religious "phenomenon." American devotion, we are told, is to "the American way of life" and not to God. It is a "civil religion," a "culture religion," a reinforcement of patriotism and political conservatism, a "religion in general" without specific doctrinal challenge or content, a materialistic creed supporting American "consumerism." According to this interpretation, there has been a notable change in American religion, but survey indicators cannot measure the phenomenon because the change—in the direction of secularization—is masked by the "civil religion" (a term introduced by sociologist Robert Bellah in a 1983 article analyzing, not the religious behavior of Americans, but presidential inauguration addresses). The most sophisticated advocates of the civil religion model cite the theories of Durkheim and Weber, the two founders of modern sociology, to support their position. Durkheim argued that religion originates in the feelings of "effervescence" by which society becomes conscious of itself in moments of enthusiasm during collective ritual. The trouble with applying Durkheim's model to contemporary Western society is that we are still faced with the question of why collective effervescence produces religious devotion in the most advanced industrialized nation in the world but not in Europe.

The civil religion model is both too complicated to describe American religion and not complicated enough. It is too complicated, according to its supporters, to admit of simple operationalization and measurement of the sort that empirically oriented scholars demand. Show us a way we might disprove your theory, the empiricists plead, because that which cannot be disproved cannot be proven; a proposition which cannot be falsified cannot be verified. But in fact the real weakness of the civil religion theory is that it is not complicated enough. It reduces American religion to an explanation which demands a day-or-night choice: either American religion is authentic, prophetic, and challenging or it is inauthentic, culture-supporting, and comforting. Such a categorizing of reality does not admit of a complex gray zone in which reality exists in a "both/and" instead of an "either/or" configuration. In as large and complex a society as the United States, both dimensions of religion almost certainly coexist both in their pure forms and in many admixtures of the two. Moreover, in a reality as complex as the human personality, religion can and probably does play roles of comfort, challenge, and perhaps both together in different social and personal situations. Although the prophet and the moralist may wish to restrict a phenomenon to day-or-night categories, the scholar should seek to understand when American religion comforts and when it challenges, with no a priori expectations that it only comforts. The data in Chapter 9 on the influence of religious imagery suggest that some images are much more likely than others to produce a compassionate religious vision.

In short, those who assert that there is change which the measures analyzed here do not detect, change in the direction of secularization, must prove the existence of such change by some technique which social science can verify. If they are unwilling to engage in such efforts at proof, then they may be playing a fascinating game, but it is not scholarship.

If we attempt to test the civil religion theory against the empirical data, we are hard put to find evidence to support it. Let us suppose, on the basis of the frequent description of it, that one of the functions of such a religion is to support conservative superpatriotism. Under such a supposition, it is reasonable to assume that those who are more devout would be more likely to want money spent on weapons and the military and less likely to want it spent on aid to underdeveloped countries. But in fact that supposition is not supported by the data in Table 10.1. There is no difference among either Catholics or Protestants between those who go to church every week and those who do not go at all in the conviction that "too little" money is being spent on defense. Moreover, among both Catholics and Protestants the weekly churchgoers are significantly (in the statistical sense) less likely to think that too much money is being spent on foreign aid. It may well be that American religion does not sufficiently challenge its members on this subject. But it is not true that religious devotion reinforces this attitude. Indeed, the opposite is true: although the majority of the devout also oppose foreign aid, they are less likely to do so than the undevout.

The theory of the civil religion is not refuted by this minor test; but neither is it supported. And if the religion of superpatriotism does not reinforce right-wing stands on the military and on foreign aid, one is permitted to wonder what it does reinforce. The flag behind the pulpit of the TV evangelist does not prove in itself that he is making converts to superpatriotic beliefs. In the absence of data to support such conversion, one might as well assume that he is preaching, not to potential converts, but to the already converted.

The criticism of American religion as "not authentic" dismisses

Table 10.1. Correlations between church attendance and foreign policy attitudes, Protestants and Catholics, 1972–1985

	Protestants	Catholics
More money for arms	.00	.00
More money for aid	.08[a]	.03[a]

Source: Pooled data, GSS, 1972–1985.

a. Difference statistically significant at .001 for Protestants, at .04 for Catholics.

the American religious phenomenon without explaining it. From the perspective of logic, what remains of European devotion might also lack authenticity. The question is not why one form of inauthenticity survives and the other apparently does not, but why the secularization model fits so much of the European data and not the American data. Why did the decline in Catholic church attendance stop in 1975 in the United States but not in Germany? It is to this kind of question that future research in the sociology of American religion must address itself, using more elaborate and sensitive social indicator measures than those presently available.

There are several ways of explaining the nonreplication of European trends in America. One is that America lacks a history of feudalism, monarchy, and an established church. Thus religion in America has never been identified with any particular side in class struggles the way it has been in Europe. "Clericalism," insofar as it exists at all, is not perceived as "the enemy" as it was and is in France, and has therefore not generated a virulent "anticlericalism" (save in certain minute portions of the population) which views religion as the enemy of freedom and progress. It is not necessary today, even in most liberal academic circles, to break with religion in order to establish one's credentials as an opponent of obscurantism, privilege, and reaction.

Moreover, on the positive side, the deliberately self-conscious pluralism which is both the official and unofficial policy of American society has created a situation in which self-definition and social location have become an important part of personal identity. If religion is about believing and belonging, if it provides a community to which people can belong and find explanation and reinforcement for the ultimate values (symbols) they share with other members of that community, then there is little in American experience to persuade most Americans that they should avoid such community and much to persuade them that they should join and be active in religious communities, to ask not "Why be religious?" but rather to ask "Why not be religious?"

A "rational choice" theory does much to explain the persistence of religion in the United States. Some 30 percent of Americans decide between their twenty-fifth and fortieth birthdays to become regular churchgoers (and this increase from 30 to 60 percent is an estimate based on age/cohort analysis), 10 percent of Americans also decide to move (back, in most cases) from religious nonidentification to religious identification. Perhaps many more make decisions, in their early and middle twenties, about continuing their original religious identification and the devotional levels of their middle teens.

In the United States more than four-fifths of those who are born Catholic and more than nine-tenths of those who are born Protestant or Jewish eventually opt for their own religious heritage. Why? I suggest that the reason for this is that in the calculus of benefits, the choice of one's own religion seems to most Americans, finally, to confer the most benefits. The choice of the religion of one's parents may suggest a certain propensity to choose the familiar because so much has been invested in the familiar, perhaps a phenomenon not unlike the decision to remain with one's original word-processing program even if other programs promise more benefits, because (quite rationally) it is calculated that the advantages of the new program do not offset the investment of startup time required to obtain skill in it. Stigler and Becker's (1977) theory of "addiction" or "consumption capital" may also be pertinent, although they were discussing "addiction" to classical music. Stated in terms of religious identification, the theory would assert that the marginal utility of time allocated to a given denomination is increased by an increase in the stock of religious capital. Thus the consumption of a given religious heritage could be said to rise with exposure to the heritage because the marginal utility of time spent on the heritage rose with exposure. Could people be said to be "addicted" to their religious heritage because they have acquired consumption capital in that heritage? It is difficult to learn the rituals, protocols, and doctrines of one religion; why bother learning another when the extra benefit does not seem all that great?

I propose the following paradigm. Most Americans are born into a religious heritage of some sort. There are five components of that heritage which may be conveniently considered: (1) a set of symbols which, *pace* Clifford Geertz, purport to explain uniquely the real, to provide answers to problems of injustice, suffering, and death; (2) a set of rituals which activate these symbols at crucial life-cycle turning points and inculcate the paradigms which the symbols can contain; (3) a community which is constituted by and transmits these symbols and rituals; (4) a heritage to pass on to one's children, should one wish; (5) a differentiation, thick or thin, from those who are not born inside the heritage.

Let us consider the schedule of benefits a person faces, say, in the middle twenties, when considering a religious decision. First of all, the community provides a pool of preferred partners, friends, marital partners, perhaps business or professional colleagues. Second, it offers familiar rituals for crucial turning points in one's life. Third, it offers symbols, usually absorbed very early in childhood, which express meaning when one is in a situation which requires meaning. Fourth, it offers various social and organizational activities which confer advantages of various sorts on its members. The more actively one engages in religious activities—up to a certain point, perhaps—the more available these resources may become. (There may also be a law of diminishing returns: attending Sunday mass may find someone a spouse, but attending daily mass may not notably increase the chances of doing so.)

In the case of each of these benefits there will be considerable cost in giving up their utility. Other partners may not respond to the most familiar interactive cues. Valuable relationship networks may be lost. It may be necessary to learn new symbols and integrate them into one's personality orientations—not an easy task in adulthood, perhaps for many not even a possible task— or to engage in unfamiliar ritual behaviors which might be distasteful. New organizational activities may involve relative strangers.

Or people may have to live without symbols, rituals, and community—or try to do so.

What are the alternative benefits on the schedule of options which would attract people to choose a heritage other than their own or, if it be possible, no heritage at all? (1) They might punish parents and church leaders with whom they are angry. (2) They might gain upward social mobility. Leaving Catholicism or Judaism to become a Protestant might provide access to elite social positions or more esteem in elite circles. (Only in the last two decades, for example, have Catholics and Jews become college presidents.) (3) They might win freedom from what they take to be the restraints, superstitions, repressions, and tyrannies inherent in their heritage and community. They can, for example, eat bacon for breakfast or (in the old days) meat on Friday; they can use the birth control pill with a clear conscience; they need not take seriously what the local pastor or priest has to say; they can ignore the pope and refuse to be worried about Israel. (4) They might become free to engage with clear conscience in pleasurable practices on which their religious heritage seems to frown or to embrace social and ethical concerns which do not preoccupy their religious leaders—when was the last time the Catholic Church launched a campaign for good government? (5) They may obtain access to a particularly desired partner—a potential spouse in most cases—who would otherwise not be available.

How do people deal with the loss of such benefits if they choose to stay within the heritage in which they are raised (normally this is the option exercised)? They may choose to ignore the restraints and the liabilities which the tradition seems to impose. For example, they may remain devoutly Catholic in their own estimation and still practice birth control because they can appeal from a church leadership which does not understand to a God who does.

This is the ordinary strategy in religious choice, since most Americans do indeed elect to remain in their own heritage. The choice becomes more desirable and hence more rational to the extent to which people are able, one way or another, to diminish the costs of the choice. Thus in 1960, 15 percent of Americans who had been raised Catholic no longer described themselves as Catholics. With the age composition of the population taken into account through age/cohort analyses, this rate has increased to 16 percent. Despite the confusion and turbulence in the Catholic church for the last quarter-century, the defection rate has not changed at all. In sum, the "familiarity" factor (or religious consumption capital)—broadly understood—explains why it seems rational, finally, for most people in the United States to opt for their own heritage.

Why, then, is it rational for Americans to be more devout than the English or the French, and the Irish to be even more devout than Americans?

One possible explanation is that a "minority" religion, that is to say one that is not state established (and in this sense all American religions are "minorities"), is likely to try harder to attract and hold its members. It thus becomes increasingly rational to stay in your tradition and reap the extra benefits that the tradition confers because of its minority status. Moreover, there may well be a relationship between the degree of religious devotion and activity in which you engage and the services which the institution (in the interests of its own self-preservation) will make available to you: if you are not a devout Catholic, you may not be able to take advantage of the parochial schools.

In the "minority" or pluralistic situation, the church may go out of its way to help find you a presentable marriage partner, more out of its way than it would in a situation where it has a near monopoly on available spouses. It is rational to take advantage of such a situation. But the variety and quality of the pool may depend to some extent on your willingness to engage in high levels of religious behavior.

For many, membership in a minority group merely intensifies the identification; that which strengthens identity is often estimated to be worth the cost, social or otherwise. The combination of symbol, ritual, and community provides a partial "identity."

A closely related explanation is that a religion attracts loyalty and devotion from its members in proportion to the thickness of its differentiation from other groups, for two reasons: ordinarily the religion will offer more services when its membership is sharply distinguished from the rest of society, and hence perhaps in jeopardy of defection; and paradoxically, the distinction is a benefit itself. Hence the more loyal people are to their heritage, the stronger the distinction and the more proudly it is professed. Conversely, in one-religion societies (either de facto or *de jure*) the differentiation is very thin, and the efforts the church perceives as necessary to attract and hold members are minimal. Hence there is less incentive to commit oneself to higher levels of religious behavior.

If a church does not perceive itself as threatened and membership in it adds little to people's identity as members of a society, if it does not differentiate its members sharply from the rest of society, then there are both lower costs and lower benefits in choosing between membership and defection, and hence less payoff for engaging in actions or professing beliefs which would link its members more closely to their church.

As a test case let us consider England, which according to measurable survey data is a notably less religious society than the United States. On the basis of the discussion above we would hypothesize that most if not all of the lower levels of "faith" and devotion will be an Anglican phenomenon and that Catholics and Protestants in England will not differ notably from Catholics in the United States in their levels of religious devotion.

Eighty-one percent of the population of Great Britain believes in God as opposed to 96 percent in the United States (Greeley, 1987). Twenty-six percent of the people of Great Britain attend church every week as opposed to 44 percent in the United States. Fifty-seven percent of Britons believe in life after death as opposed to 70 percent of Americans. But there is no difference between Catholics and Protestants in these two countries in belief in God and life after death or in church attendance: 42 percent of the Protestants in both countries go to church every week, as do 50 percent of the Catholics. Approximately 70 percent of both religious groups in both countries believe in life after death. Ninety-eight percent of the Catholics in both countries believe in God, 94 percent of the Protestants. The lower levels of religiousness in Great Britain are purely an Anglican phenomenon.

Unintentionally, perhaps, American life seems to reinforce the loyalty factor which Hout and I (1988) found latent in both political affiliation and church attendance. The factor is both discrete and continuous. There is a threshold of loyalty that people apparently elect to cross or not to cross in their late teens or early twenties. Once they choose to be a religious and/or political alienate at that threshold, they are likely to remain so for the rest of their lives. On the other hand, if they cross the threshold, even to the extent of identifying with a political party by reporting that they are independents "leaning" toward one party or the other or by attending church at least once a year, then their level of political and/or religious affiliation is likely to increase over a lifetime. Perhaps age makes people more conservative and more in need of firm guidelines. Or perhaps with the passage of time people become more aware of the complexity of human existence and hence more tolerant of the imperfections of their church and party and more in need of clearly marked guideposts. Or perhaps they want to be able to pass on such useful guideposts to their children so that they can chart a safe and happy path through life's confusions. Or perhaps all three explanations come to the same thing: some guideposts and some community to set up the posts and maintain the signs on them are better than none.

These possible explanations can be converted into operational measures; but social scientists will begin to work on such measures only when they are convinced that religion is not losing its importance in American life and hence is still worth studying as a major component of social structure and of the glue which holds the society, however precariously at times, together.

The null hypothesis that religious attitudes and behaviors in America are not changing has not been appreciably weakened by the survey data available to us. Whatever may be said in theory about the success of science in its battle with religion, religion does not in general seem to have been notably weakened in the United States during the past half-century, insofar as we are able to measure its strength from survey items.

The secularization model, which has never been confirmed by the data and has often been disproved—as in this book—nonetheless remains as strong as ever in scholarly and journalistic circles, unshaken and apparently unshakable. Students of religion will be not surprised. They know a religion when they see one. They know that religious faith is difficult if not impossible to disprove. Secularization as a theory itself confirms the stability model.

References

American Institute of Public Opinion (AIPO) (Princeton Research Center). 1982, 1983, 1984, 1985. *Religion in America*. Princeton, N.J.

Bellah, Robert. 1983. *Varieties of Civil Religion*. San Francisco: Harper & Row.

Caplow, Theodore, Howard M. Baher, Bruce A. Chadwick, and Dwight Hoover. 1983. *All Faithful People: Change and Continuity in Middletown's Religion*. Minneapolis: University of Minnesota Press.

Duncan, Otis Dudley. 1985. "Rasch Measurement: Further Examples and Discussion." In *Surveying Subjective Phenomena*, vol. 2, ed. Charles F. Turner and Elizabeth Martin, pp. 367–403. New York: Russell Sage Foundation.

Geertz, Clifford. 1966. "Religion as a Culture System." In *Anthropological Approaches to the Study of Religion*, ed. Michael Bonton, pp. 1–46. New York: Praeger.

General Social Surveys (GSS). 1972–1987. Raw data available in James A. Davis and Tom W. Smith. 1987. "General Social Surveys, 1972–1987: Cumulative Codebook." Storrs, Conn.: Roper Center for Public Opinion Research.

Glazer, Nathan, and Daniel Patrick Moynihan. 1963. *Beyond the Melting Pot*. Cambridge, Mass.: MIT Press.

Glenn, Norval. 1987. "No Religion Respondents." *Public Opinion Quarterly*, 51:293–315.

Greeley, Andrew. 1987. *Religion and Values: Three English-Speaking Nations*. Chicago: NORC.

————. 1978. *Religion: A Secular Theory*. New York: Free Press/Macmillan.

Greeley, Andrew, and Michael Hout. 1988. "Musical Chairs: Patterns of Denominational Change." *Sociology and Social Research*, 72:75–86.

Greeley, Andrew, William C. McCready, and Kathleen McCourt. 1976.

Catholic Schools in a Declining Church. Kansas City, Mo.: Andrews and McMeel.

Greeley, Andrew, and William E. McManus. 1987. *Catholic Financial Contributions.* Chicago: Thomas More Press.

Greeley, Andrew, and Peter H. Rossi. 1965. *The Education of Catholic Americans.* Chicago: Aldine Press.

Hay, David, and A. Morisy. 1978. "Reports of Ecstatic Paranormal or Religious Experience in Great Britain and the United States—a Comparison of Trends." *Journal for the Scientific Study of Religion,* 17:255–268.

Herberg, Will. 1960. *Protestant Catholic Jew.* Garden City, N.Y.: Anchor Books.

Hout, Michael, and Andrew Greeley. 1987. "The Center Doesn't Hold." *American Sociological Review,* 52:325–345.

James, William. 1902. *The Varieties of Religious Experience.* New York: Modern Library.

Johnson, Robert Alan. 1985. *Religious Associative Marriages.* New York: Praeger.

Kelly, Dean M. 1977. *Why Conservative Churches Are Growing.* New York: Harper & Row.

Knoke, David, and Michael Hout. 1974. "Social and Demographic Factors in American Political Party Preferences, 1952–1972." *American Sociological Review,* 39:700–713.

Lipset, Seymour Martin. "The Elections, the Economy, and Public Opinion: 1984." *PS,* 18:28–38.

Lopatto, Paul. 1985. *Religion and the Presidential Election.* New York: Praeger.

McCready, William, and Andrew Greeley. 1975. *Ultimate Values of Americans.* Beverly Hills: Sage Publications.

Morgan, James, et al. 1962. *Income and Welfare in the United States.* New York: McGraw-Hill.

———. 1979. *Results of Two National Surveys in Philanthropic Activities.* Ann Arbor: University of Michigan Press.

Olson, P. Richard, Joe A. Suddeth, Patricia J. Peterson, and Claudia Egelhoff. 1985. "Hallucinations of Widowhood." *Journal of the American Geriatric Society,* 33:543.

Otto, Rudolph. 1952. *The Idea of the Holy.* London: Oxford University Press.

Rasch, Georg. 1960. *Probabilistic Models for Some Intelligence and Attainment Tests.* Copenhagen: Danish Institute for Educational Research.

Roof, Wade Clark, and William McKinney. 1987. *American Mainline Religion*. New Brunswick, N.J.: Rutgers University Press.

Smith, Tom W. 1987. "Classifying American Denominations." Unpublished paper. Chicago: NORC.

———. 1988. "Counting Flocks and Lost Sheep: Trends in Religious Preference since World War II." Unpublished paper. Chicago: NORC.

Stigler, George, and Gary Becker. 1977. "De Gustibus Non Est Disputandum." *American Economic Review*, 67:76–90.

White, Arthur H. 1986. *The Charitable Behavior of Americans*. New York: Yankelovich, Shelly and White.

Index

Abortion, 37, 82, 92, 93, 99

Afterlife: belief in, in America, 15–16, 20, 33, 66, 116; belief in, in other countries, 15–16, 126; images of, 15, 101–104; and mystical experiences, 107

American Institute of Public Opinion (AIPO) survey data, 8; on belief in God, 13–15; on belief in afterlife, 15; on biblical literalism, 16, 17; on denominational affiliations, 19–20, 22, 24–28; on importance of religion, 38–40, 62, 115; on religious behaviors, 40, 42–46, 58, 60, 67–68

Baptists, 10, 28, 33, 38, 89–90, 103. *See also* Protestants

Becker, Gary, 122

Bellah, Robert, 118

Berger, Peter, 6

Bible: belief in literal truth of, 16–20, 33, 37, 112, 113, 115; frequency of reading of, 19, 20, 115; belief in divine influence on, 116

Birth control encyclical (1968): effect on Catholics' attitudes toward papal authority, 20; effect on Catholics' church attendance, 47–52, 55, 112, 115; effect on Catholics' financial contributions, 70, 71–75. *See also* Papal authority; Second Vatican Council

Caplow, Theodore, 117

Catholic Digest study, 9, 15

Catholics: and biblical literalism, 18–19,

20, 112, 115; and papal authority, 20, 72, 93, 101; and denominational affiliations, 22, 24–28, 33, 40, 60–61, 122; patterns of church attendance, 44–56, 68, 72, 74, 112, 115, 121, 126–127; political affiliation, 50–53, 80–86, 87, 116; interreligious attitudes, 62–64, 115; financial contributions, 67, 68–75, 112; sexual attitudes, 72–73, 90, 92–93, 103; political attitudes, 76, 87–90, 100–101, 114, 116, 120; economic and social success, 76, 77–80, 82, 85, 93, 113, 116, 124; and abortion, 82, 92, 93; religious images among, 102–104; American vs. English, 126–127. *See also* Birth control encyclical; Second Vatican Council

Church attendance: as measure of religious commitment, 3, 40, 42, 66; among unaffiliated, 33; patterns among Protestants, 36, 37, 44–46, 55–56; effect of age on, 42, 44–47, 54–55; patterns among Catholics, 44–56, 68, 72, 74, 112, 115, 121, 126–127; correlation with political affiliation, 50–54, 80–86, 87, 116, 127; stability of American patterns, 56, 57, 116, 117

Churches: membership in organizations related to, 37, 57, 60, 65, 66, 116; financial contributions to, 67–75, 112

Denominational affiliations: importance of, in America, 21, 40–41, 52–54, 121–125; measures of, 21–22; among

Papal authority, 20, 48, 72, 93, 101, 124

Political affiliation: correlation with church attendance, 50–54, 80–86, 87, 116, 127; and people's images of God, 98–99

Pope John Paul II, 93

Pope Paul VI, 47, 51

Prayer, 36, 57–58, 66; increase in frequency of, 59, 60, 65, 115

Presbyterians, 22, 24, 27, 35, 80, 90, 103. *See also* Protestants

Protestants, 9–10; changes in religion of, 8, 20, 112–114; and biblical literalism, 19–20; and denominational affiliations, 22, 24–28, 33–38, 40, 60–62, 112, 122; patterns of church attendance, 54–55, 127; interreligious attitudes, 62–64, 115; financial contributions, 67, 68–69, 71, 74, 75; political attitudes, 76, 80–82, 83–86, 87–90, 116, 120; economic and social success, 77–80; and abortion, 82, 93; sexual attitudes, 90, 92–93, 103; religious images among, 100, 102, 103; American vs. English, 126–127

Rasch, Georg, 51

Religion: role of, 1–2, 119; conflict of, with science, 2, 6, 113, 128; indicators of, 5, 8–11, 67, 94, 111, 114–115, 116, 117; and politics, 6, 50–54, 76, 80–86, 90, 119–120; secularization model for, 6, 7, 11, 12, 115, 118–121, 128; stability model for, 7, 8, 20, 40–41, 115–117, 127–128; as system of symbols, 7, 10, 94–96, 121, 123; correlation with age, 10–11, 22–24, 40, 106–107, 110, 127; imagery of, 10, 96–111, 119; in Europe, 13, 15, 16, 21, 42, 54, 59, 117, 125;

importance of, to Americans, 38–40, 54, 127–128; prayer as measure of, 57–58, 65–66; and mystical experiences, 59–60, 65, 104–111, 115; denominational changes in, 60–62, 112; in Third World, 117–118. *See also* Catholics; Jews; Protestants

Religious imagery, 10, 96–111, 119

Religious nonaffiliation, 23, 28–33

Roof, Wade Clark, 21, 35

Rossi, Peter H., 20, 25

Second Vatican Council, 6–7, 113; effect on Catholics' acceptance of biblical literalism, 18, 20, 112; effect on Catholics' church attendance, 42, 47, 50; effect on interreligious attitudes, 62; effect on religious images, 101. *See also* Birth control encyclical

Secularization model: supporters of, 2, 3–4, 116, 118–119, 128; lack of supporting data for, 8, 11–12, 42, 65–66, 75, 117, 128; in Europe, 117–118, 121; and "civil religion," 118–121

Sexual attitudes, 72–73, 90, 92–93, 102, 103–104, 115

Smith, Tom W., 38

Stigler, George, 122

Survey Research Center (SRC) data (University of Michigan), 8, 16–17, 19, 26–27, 62, 67–68

Thomas, W. I., 111

Weber, Max, 77, 118

White, Arthur H., 67

Yankelovich study, 67, 73